MIND
MOVIES

Douglas A. Cox

MIND MOVIES

Douglas A. Cox
1000 N. Green Valley Parkway
Suite 440-392
Henderson, NV 89074
United States of America
Website: www.DougCoxOnline.com
Email: DougCox22@cox.net

Editing by Sharon Norman

Book Layout & Design by Linda A. Bell
Bell Creative Studio

BIOGRAPHY & AUTOBIOGRAPHY/personal memoirs/mind movies/ Douglas A. Cox - 1st. ed.

ISBN-13: 978-1727185898
ISBN-10: 1727185897

Printed in the United States of America

Disclaimer
The purpose of this book is to educate, motivate, and inspire. The author shall have neither liability nor responsibility to any person or entity with respect to any loss or damage caused or alleged to be caused directly or indirectly by the information contained in this book.

CONTENTS

CONTENTS

CONTENTS

Author's Invitation

For many years I have been writing to you… In fact, it's more than that. I have been writing to you, for you, with you and about you!

I have been blest by visiting the most wonderful places and meeting the most amazing people, both famous and infamous and I have decided that it was time we share this great adventure.

Here you will come face to face with the wonderful people, artists and stars I have had the good fortune to know. You will also meet my four-legged friends:

Holly, Goldilocks, Mike, Elvis, Cabo, Daisy, Tank, Three O'clock On The Nose, Leo and the one and only Cricket.

When a reader/subscriber of my weekly column, *The Desert Wind,* wrote about one of my adventures, she said that my writing created the very best "Mind Movies!" That very kind testimonial inspired the title of this book.

We are all so busy now, so swallowed up by our technology, I have created a book that asks and answers the question: "Have you got a moment?"

Come away with me then… As we Ride Together on the Desert Wind!

Doug Cox, aka "Tigger"

See photo gallery on my website:
www.dougcoxonline.com/mind-movies-photos

SCENE ONE

Looking for a Smile

● ● ● ● ● ● ● ●

Strange times in our great nation; in a whole bunch of living, I have never felt the tension and vitriol pouring forth from the glass box that is supposed to keep us entertained and informed. Time for a smile! In fact, laughter might just be the Rx for all of us but where to look?

We were watching the Weather Channel here in our home in Las Vegas, when the crawl across the bottom of the screen caught my eye… My first impression as a writer was that someone had misspelled a word or two and the editor had failed to catch it. By the time I was zoned in on the message, it had disappeared from the screen. So, I camped out to watch for it just in case it came back around and sure enough here it was: In small type, with no fanfare it simply said… "Do you have *looth* or *mithing* teeth?" Could I have read that right? Too late, it was gone again. Next time I caught it: "Do you have *looth* or *mithing* teeth?" Well I started laughing so hard that my wife came in to

9

check on my wellbeing. We were being entertained by a simple, probably inexpensive, advertisement for a local dentist. Whatever the budget, I had to put it right up there with Budweiser's Clydesdale football game or the rough and rugged *"Cowboys Herding Cats"* commercial…

I always enjoyed Red Skelton, Jonathan Winters and Flip Wilson, two of whom I knew very well. They were funny *with us* and not at our expense. They used their intellect instead of profanity, to share a smile with us. Let's check out the funny papers, boot up some Marx Brothers, practice our Inspector Clouseau, talk like a pirate and subscribe to the Looney Tunes channel.

We watch together!
Tigger

SCENE TWO

Birthdays

● ● ● ● ● ● ● ●

The evening put itself to bed, warm, sultry and still. Next morning the temperature dropped a full twenty degrees and the day came to life, cool, crisp, breezy and fresh. The fragrance of fields, flowers, trees and farms, filled the morning air. In Amish Country, autumn was being born.

I am in Lancaster, PA, a town founded in 1729. During this week, in 1777, our nation was also being born. For *one day*, September 27, 1777, with the Continental Congress in retreat from the British invaders in Philadelphia, the Capital of the New Nation was moved to Lancaster, PA. Lancaster is one of the oldest inland towns in the United States.

A hint at the history of this beautiful place: The famous explorer, Meriwether Lewis, came here to learn the art of surveying and map making, that would document the Corp of Discovery journey through the heart of this wild and unexplored continent.

Here also were born the Conestoga Wagon, the Pennsylvania Long Rifle and the incredible NORTHSTAR Class of September 2016. Nineteen very bright locals came together, in an old farmhouse, to share, grow and look to the continued building of our Nation. Who wouldn't love a state with names like, Bird-in-Hand, Toad Suck, Hump Tulips and my kids favorite… Intercourse.

God Bless America!
Tigger

SCENE THREE

One Eyed Jacks

● ● ● ● ● ● ●

It was about 8 weeks ago when I noticed a tiny dot on my lower left eyelid. With years of experience under my belt, I headed for my dermatologist and he confirmed my suspicions. This was skin cancer.

Together we decided to remove that rascal with MOHS surgery. To clean it up, took about 8 hours of hard labor on the part of my physician and friend, Doctor Mac. I walked away with the confidence that he got it all! He took my complete lower eyelid with it but that is the power of MOHS, you don't quit until you are clear! That was day one. On day two I headed for an ocular reconstructive surgeon to begin the process of putting me back together. That was a brief two-hour procedure, under general anesthesia, in which this wizard took a little bit here and a little bit there, pasted me back together and stitched my left eye closed.

My eye remained closed for thirty days, at which

time we celebrated the "Eye Opening Oscars!" In the meantime, my pirate appearance was a great source of entertainment for friends and family alike. I share this with you, not to alarm you but to encourage you to use your sunscreen, wear a fine, foxy hat and for heaven's sake, have regular check-ups with your dermatologist.

I have a lot more waves to ride and I am counting on you being out there with me!

We Ride Together,
One Eyed Tigger

SCENE FOUR

The Scarf

• • • • • • • •

My readers, who also view my Wednesday Video Blogs, know that I almost always wear a scarf! After all, no self-respecting cowboy would ride off without one.

Some years ago, our friend and totem pole partner Nanook, invited us "North to Alaska," to share in Hooligan's Weekend. That's the weekend that the ice breaks up and comes downriver, making way for the hooligan fish and salmon to return. No way could we pass up four days and nights camped out on an island in the middle of the Susitna River, in the heart of Alaska. Only one rule: *"No Drinking once the sun goes down!"* Well it worked out just fine. You see, at that time of year the sun dips behind the horizon for about four minutes and then re-appears again for another 23-plus hours.

On the fourth day of feasting and merriment under the noonday sun, we all agreed that we could use a bath, so all fourteen of us clung on to Rick's Zodiac boat like seals and motored on up to Gabbert's Fish Camp for a steam bath. Imagine my surprise, when we hauled out onto the bank and our band of pirates and pirettes, leaped onto the sand and began shedding their clothing… All of their clothing! When I saw the guests at the fish camp grabbing their cameras and jockeying for a spot at the window, I thought quickly and realized. *"Hey! I'm Doug Cox, I can't just go running around naked in the wilderness,"* so… I left my scarf on…

Tigger

SCENE FIVE

The Light

● ● ● ● ● ● ● ●

Three Hundred years ago, in 1716, on the east coast of what would become America, a lighthouse was built in Boston Harbor. "Boston Light," as it is called, is an incredible piece of our Nation's history. Standing tall and proud, she has faithfully warned mariners of the hidden dangers lurking beneath her turbulent waters.

O' how I wish the Fresnel lens was polished and the light would shine in the darkness of our time for those of us patriots who still love our nation so dearly. Time, once again, to heed the warning of the Boston Light. *Rocky shoals ahead,* prejudice and violence; *Rough Seas,* hardened hearts and bitter words. These ill winds must not remain the basis of our fellowship and discourse. Where once the passion for "One Nation" was our inspiration and love of God and Country was our promise, we now sail in the perilous darkness of hatred.

May the sweep of the Boston Light wash across our beloved land once again and become the beacon for reason, honor and respect.

Tears in my eyes, hand on my heart,
Tigger

SCENE SIX

Eyes

● ● ● ● ● ● ● ●

Night was falling and on the darkened pathway, I said softly to my wife, *"Did you see that?"* As the light was disappearing on our evening walk, I had spotted a very tiny snake on the ground. "How did you see it?" She asked.

It is a question I have heard before in regard to my flower and creature photos. *"How do you find all of these flowers and critters that you capture in your photographs?"* My answer is simple but very important: "I am guided..." When I walk the many miles I do in a day, week or month, I try to focus on the path or trail ahead, so that I do not trip, stumble or fall. Try though I may, to maintain this vigilance, I am constantly alerted to objects both left and right, above and below, behind and before, that are often very still, tiny and nearly obscure. For this gift, my Native American friends have given me a nickname, *"Calls His Eyes..."* Because, after listening, watching and photographing the nature that surrounds me for so long, I have trained my senses to see those things others might not or do not! As many of you have revealed to me the secrets of your profession, your knowledge or discipline, my joy is revealing for you my discoveries.

Happy news... You can do this too. Before you set out on a walk or hike, take a moment to still your mind. Turn off the flashing invasion of your television at least fifteen minutes before you set forth and then go, eyes open, mind open, wide open. Don't try so hard to find things, just enjoy the time, exercise and experience and things will find you.

Tigger

SCENE SEVEN

North

● ● ● ● ● ● ● ●

At the very topmost point of the great Pacific Ocean, where the needle on the compass points to N, there is a magnificent inlet, leading into a deep, green and mysterious body of water, known as Resurrection Bay. It is home to silver salmon, whales, sea lions, sea otters and all types of Aquarian life. No less the creatures of the air, from tiny murres, to puffins, ducks, geese, cormorants, seagulls and the proudest of them all, Bald Eagles! This last week I was given a grand tour of the bay by my Totem Brother, Rick *"Nanook"* Thornton.

Aboard the *"Stacy K,"* with Rick at the helm, we covered nearly every inch of this magnificent bay, sharing stories and folklore about the first people who were here long before the white man came in search of gold, only to fall in love with the people and land. These brief summer days are too early for northern lights but just right for the midnight sun. Out on the bluff, at Rick's home, overlooking Turnagain Arm with the mighty Alaska range in the distance, we shared the warmth of a wood fire and the fellowship and memories of Alaskan's I have come to know.

I urge you, my beloved readers, to take inspiration from this simple message and make just such memories for yourself, your family and your loved ones. Wherever you now reside, there is history and nature calling out for you, to cook-out, camp-out, dine-out and share the love and memories of life. You can do it… I know, because Rick and I became friends over fifty years ago at a Redken Challenge of Success Seminar and we just decided to make it stick…

Naglikpok… I love my friends!
Tigger

SCENE EIGHT

Meep Meep

● ● ● ● ● ● ● ●

Here in Green Valley, a community near Las Vegas, we are having our annual invasion of grasshoppers. They are cute little gray guys and festoon the desert floor around our home. As I started up the trail for my daily adventure, the afternoon was warm, breezy and glorious. I was on the first leg up the hill, when I noticed this little cartoon character moving along just ahead of me, and no more than five feet to my side. If I slowed down he slowed down, if I sped up, he stayed right in formation.

Now I'm sure you know that most wild critters don't take kindly to humans, so I was mighty surprised and curious about his reason for hiking along with me. And then I got it. This industrious road runner was sharing the trail with me, so that I could flush out the grasshoppers for his pre-Thanksgiving feast.

Given the changes in the winds of American politics, it also came to me that this might be a fine example for our leaders, in Washington, to put their differences aside and cooperate in the service of our nation.

If you would enjoy seeing the latest stories and photos from my collection just email dougcox22@cox.net and put "Flowers!" in the subject line. I would be honored to share.

Meep-Meep!
Tigger

See photo of this roadrunner on my website:
www.dougcoxonline.com/mind-movies-photos

SCENE NINE

Pathway

● ● ● ● ● ● ● ●

Each morning, when I arise, I like to head out and climb the hill that lies behind our desert home. The City Lights Trail is a winding gravel path, that zig-zags upward to the crest of the hill. From on high, the view of the Las Vegas valley is astounding, but that is only the cherry on the top of the adventure. The pathway has become my gymnasium, my treadmill, my source of cardiovascular inspiration, trainer and more.

Because the bed of the path is made of crushed rock and gravel, it is an uneven, slippery slope to manage. On my first ascent, I found myself sliding, puffing and pausing frequently, as I struggled to reach the summit. But now, in my third month, my breathing and heart rate are smooth and relaxed. (112/62) My muscles seem to celebrate the elevation with each step.

But wait, there's more! My trail/coach is beginning to strengthen my mind as well. To keep from slipping on the gravel, I find myself looking up and focusing carefully on the terrain ahead. My eyes see the obstacles and guide each possible footfall. In doing this, my vision, focus and mental coordination have improved measurably. My balance is steady and confident; Mind body and spirit… and all for free. What is your pathway to health and vigor?

Tigger

SCENE TEN

Stretched

● ● ● ● ● ● ● ●

Sometimes I feel like a Cowboy in two worlds. I came in with the pony express and now I travel out on a Boeing 787 Dreamliner. I was raised on *"please and thank you"* and now *"you're welcome,"* has been replaced with *"no problem man!"* Was I really a problem?

Unlike our friends, who have recently opened the beautiful *"Copper Cat,"* bookstore, these brick-and-mortar literary bastions are disappearing and reading is done on smarter-than-me phones, if at all. A campfire and a lone guitar have now become a shrieking electronic band and the creaking leather of saddle horses at tether, has been replaced with the roar of four wheelers, while the fragrance of sage has given way to the smell of exhaust. The once crystal blue sky above my camp, is now crisscrossed with jet trails. A hazy brown layer of something produced in a big city, some miles away, creates a strange and eerie sunset.

Did I mention how happy I am to be here, to stretch and experience all of this? Ever watch a cat arise from its twelve hours of slumber? First thing they do is streeeeeeetch! Ever watch a marathon runner warmup? They go through some incredible stretching to prepare for the twenty-six miles ahead. I am honored to be alive, excited and ready for the new day, the new era, the brave new world! And… I am honored to share it with you.

We Ride Together!
Tigger

SCENE ELEVEN

Boots and Saddles

● ● ● ● ● ● ● ●

If you were to GOOGLE the title of this Desert Wind, you would find that "Boots and Saddles" is a famous bugle call, commanding horse soldiers to mount up and line up! You may also find a television series, a very old western movie and a bar in New York City. For me, today, it is a call to *thanks* for a wonderful gift and a great new adventure.

If you view my blogs on youtube, you have heard of my love for The Neel Ranch in Colorado. Mark and K.C. Neel, the owners, are beloved friends. On my most recent visit, Mark, in conversation asked… *"What size shoe do you wear?"* Once confirmed, my friend disappeared into the belly of the house and returned carrying a boot bag. I recognized the logo immediately and exclaimed, *"Lucchese, right?"* He sat back down and began to share a most wonderful story.

Mark's grandfather had for years before his passing, gone to the Lucchese factory to order a custom pair of boots. The boots in Mark's hand were to be his last pair. Unfortunately, he passed away before he could break them in. Ordered twenty-seven years ago and stashed in his grandson's closet, they had waited all those years to find a new home and a new owner. During our lives, we all receive a number of gifts. But to a cowboy, there is simply nothing like receiving a special pair of boots. When I mount up for the first time, to ride the Spring Range, I will be proudly wearing a special piece of Colorado history.

Thank you from the bottom of my heart for this wonderful gift of love and memories.

We Ride Together!
Tigger

SCENE TWELVE

Old Hickory

● ● ● ● ● ● ● ●

From the second floor balcony of the grand white home, the notes of a guitar spill out across Old Hickory Lake. The fragrance of the fresh water and what smelled like honeysuckle perfume, filled the evening air. The setting sun created a beautiful orange glow, the kind that artists only dream of capturing. We are in Old Hickory, Tennessee and I have been invited to this historic place to share both time and spirit with sweet friends both old and new.

I love my autumn tours and I particularly love to present my SPIRITSONG retreat. From The Strawberry Lodge in the Sierra Nevada Mountains of California, The Grand Mesa, in Colorado, The Bob Marshall Wilderness, in Montana, a historic farm house in Lancaster County, PA, to this home once owned by the country legend, Whispering Bill Anderson, every stop and every adventure has been a joy!

Wanda and Chip have opened their beautiful home and

hearts to us. For some of us in attendance, the canyons have been deep and the climb through life and loss a steep one. I can't wait to share and as I always do, learn more than I teach.

Love is the answer,
Tigger

SCENE THIRTEEN

Sermon-Song

● ● ● ● ● ● ● ●

I love music, always have. I've come through my days in radio and the recording business, to know that each of us perceives the music that we hear, very, very, differently. Some of us just love the beat, while others love the lyrics or the melody. Nature has always been my church and music has often been my sermon. I didn't realize it, until one day when a new client picked me up at the airport to drive me to our program. On the way, he took a long look at my hair, beard and cowboy attire and finally asked the question that was simmering in his mind. *"So, you're a songwriter eh?"*

"Yes, sir." I replied. He then proceeded to tell me that rock music was the gate to hell and that he hoped I wasn't going to use any of it in my presentation. As I often do, I asked him if he might show me how songs and music seemed so frightening. He reached over and tuned in a local radio station and wouldn't you know they were playing *"Make it with you,"* by David Gates.

"There," he exclaimed, *"This singer is trying to get my daughter in bed with him."*

"Perhaps," I said but I was hearing something quite different.

"Yeah… Well show me!" I was hearing the Sermon on the Mount. He gave me the strangest look and said prove it! Imagine a mount of olives and a very special messenger calling his most trusted disciples to join him. *"Hey, have you ever tried really reaching out for the other side or maybe climbing on rainbows, well baby here goes. Though you don't know me well and every little thing only time will tell, if you believe the things that I do… Then we'll see it through, I want to make it with you."* He pulled the car over to the side of the road, sat still for a long moment and then he said softly, *"I'm beginning to look forward to your presentation this evening."*

"Me too," I replied….
Tigger

SCENE FOURTEEN

Retreat

• • • • • • • •

The great naturalist, John Muir said: *"The clearest way into the universe, is through a forest wilderness."* I am prepared to taste that adventure once again. I am in the Poconos Mountains in Pennsylvania. These ancient, forested treasures, crafted by the Master's Hand, are a place of true refuge and retreat. Walk away from cities and towns and cool yourself from the late summer heat, in a crystalline blue lake. Rest well and deep beneath a billion stars and then awaken to the alarm of crickets. Share your sunrise with the squirrels and the white tail deer. Refresh your face in the rainbow-mist of a towering waterfall and give thanks for these incredible blessings and all for the price of a commitment and a climb.

Today, I will conclude my sojourn with a long, silent walk down the valley, to the sounds and sights of civilization once again. Split Rock awaits, with life-long partners and brand-new friends to share.

Together, we will change the world by improving ourselves…

Tigger

SCENE FIFTEEN

The King

• • • • • • • •

In our neighborhood and in most residential areas in our country, you will find security signs stuck into the ground in our front yards. These postings warn that anyone entering these premises will be videotaped, reported to the police, tied to a cactus and force-fed mint tea! It is clear that we want to be safe and secure on our properties.

Why would it be then that someone, dare I say some *fool,* who either hates or more than likely is afraid of snakes, killed one of these super heroes, right on the sidewalk near our home? This California King Snake is one of the most courageous and valuable neighbors we could have. Did you know that this little warrior will confront, battle, kill and devour any rattlesnake that crosses his path? In fact he or she will eliminate many of the things that you would wish away from your yard.

King snakes come in many colors, from a sleek black and

white beauty, to the "red next to black is a friend to Jack" variety. I am all for protecting my family and myself but I do not feel that the answer is to destroy anything and everything that we don't understand or that frightens us. What goes around comes around and somewhere on Doug's Mountain there is a rattlesnake awaiting the arrival of the assassin who took the life of one of our most valuable guardians.

Fears do not just go away… They are displaced by new, fresh and valuable information!

Thanks for sharing,
Tigger

SCENE SIXTEEN

Sugar

● ● ● ● ● ● ● ●

Hot! No other way to describe it. For those of us who live in the beautiful southwestern desert, we know what to expect. 105, that's cinchy. Above 105 it's hot, even for us. What we know that outsiders do not, is that this heat is the way of the desert summer.

The searing oven paints the sky a very special turquois blue. Scents that the hills have hidden away for the winter and spring, begin to exhale into the morning breeze. Rosemary, Creosote, Mojave Yucca, Juniper and Manzanita are a cowboy's perfume. Crouching in the shade of an ancient Joshua tree, the north wind brushes my sweat stained face. From the south, the first hint of monsoon shows in the dancing clouds. To the east, the Grand Canyon calls to river rafters and to the west, on the very tips of the sheep range, the last of winter's powdered sugar is disappearing.

These are wonderful days to share a climb up Doug's mountain with my friends the antelope squirrels. They don't even come out to run and play until the summer sun reaches its peak. If these are desert chipmunks, I must be a desert rat and this is *The Desert Wind!*

Bless you for sharing,
Tigger

SCENE SEVENTEEN

Showtime

● ● ● ● ● ● ● ●

My first impression was that the lighting left something to be desired. The costumes seemed to be understated, to say the least. His entrance was a total surprise but I passed it off as an attempt to be a part of this new and often strange world.

His first steps, as he came toward us, were nothing that I expected. No plié or pirouette. No arabesque or grand jetė, not even a simple turn out. His appearance was such, that I began to wonder about the company's wardrobe, dressing and make-up departments. This was definitely not *"Classical"* or *"Modern"* but the setting and scenery were real enough.

It was not until the *"Danseur"* stepped forward and held out my car keys, that I realized my mistake. This was "Valet…"

Pas de deux?
Tigger

SCENE EIGHTEEN

Front Story

● ● ● ● ● ● ● ●

Today, whether it is about a star, a politician or a neighbor, it seems that everyone wants to know the back story. They want the dirt, the gossip, the nasty little secrets. This story may just be a disappointment for you!

Many years ago, when I worked for Atlantic Records, I was fortunate enough to travel to Miami Florida for the company's annual convention. Try to imagine Aretha Franklin, Bobby Darin, CSN&Y, Buffalo Springfield and Otis Redding, all in one place.

I had been assigned to meet a gentleman from across the pond, by the name of Robert Stigwood, to shepherd his new artists throughout America, promoting their careers and their recordings. His group? *"The Bee Gees!"*

After a very exciting convention, I had the honor of escorting the Brothers Gibb onto an American Airlines flight and off to the west coast. To my great joy, I found these incredible young composer/vocalists, to be the most courteous gentlemen I had ever met. They all wanted to sit by the window, take photos and look out upon America. They were the masters of *"please"* and *"thank you"* and as the years passed, they never changed.

Throughout their incredible fame and success, The Bee Gees have remained as enthusiastic and well-mannered as the day we first met. Watching *"The Bee Gees,"* One Night Only, on PBS, I loved knowing that I was truly watching the good guys!

Tigger

SCENE NINETEEN

For the Record

● ● ● ● ● ● ● ●

Do you own some old 45 RPM records? If so why? Why do they matter to you? Why do you keep records that you can no longer play?

My friend, Ian Gavet, posted something on Facebook that got me thinking… Why do we keep these relics and why do we remember these songs and lyrics? The answer is, they are a very real part of our hearts and histories. When I was in the radio and recording business, I met some famous folks and it was a pleasure. But today, it is the artists and writers whose voices, music and recordings were never given a chance, that I remember; the folks who put their lives and souls into songs that they believed would be the next big hit.

I would like to share one such story. *"Falling in Love Again"* by Ted Mulry, was a song sent to me by a friend from RCA records in Australia. I liked the 70's song and agreed to try to get it played on the radio. We got it started in Southern California and audiences loved the song. Imagine my surprise when I was told to forget about it. All I could think about was the disappointment in the heart of my new friend Ted Mulry, who had his hopes and dreams spinning around, at 45 RPM, on that little piece of vinyl.

I'll bet you have a song or a poem that you wish the world could share! How about this… You tell me about your oldest, most favorite 45 record (famous or not) and you can Google the song, "Falling in Love Again" by Ted Mulry and listen to it online. Let me know what you think! We lost Ted in 2001 but his music lives on.

Save me a dance!
Tigger

SCENE TWENTY

Instant

● ● ● ● ● ● ● ●

I love football. I enjoyed playing it in high school and for years I have watched it faithfully. It was a crisp fall California afternoon and we, still in our jammies, were watching a football game on T.V. For me it was a Sunday joy with my kids.

I remember it like it was yesterday. John Madden was explaining to us a new feature of the game called *"Instant Replay."* As we watched John's usual clear explanation of this new technological addition to the game, I found myself caught in the revelation. So, when my daughter Barbee looked up and asked, *"What do you think daddy?"* My reply was: *"We will never see the game of football the same way again little one!"* Up until that *moment* the game had been ours. We watched every play intently, because we didn't want to miss a *moment* of our beloved pastime. Every play, every tackle every touchdown was something that we shared. We were truly a part of the *moment* in which it happened. Now, in an instant, that *moment* was put in the hands of producers and sponsors.

We no longer had to be a part of the *moment.* We could head out to the fridge for a beer or some guacamole. After all we could always watch the re-play, later-on. It wasn't a game anymore. On the field, the officiating crew was no longer in charge or even trusted by the players. There is no such thing as a moment later on… Always remember, the moment is now!

I love football…
Tigger#22

SCENE TWENTY-ONE

P.F.D.

• • • • • • • •

His fighter plane hit the surface of the water at more than one hundred miles an hour. The impact with the cold, roiling sea, put out the fire immediately but left in its wake his need to survive in the mighty Pacific Ocean. You have just crash landed on the largest and deepest ocean basin on earth. What do you do now?

Each summer, here in Nevada, we learn on the news about a drowning in our beautiful Lake Mead. It could be a child but sometimes it is an able bodied adult... Why? The answer is, panic! I have a different word for it but I would be considered very politically incorrect, if I were to insert it here. Anyone who prepares for a trip on or in the water should know:

How to swim... Don't go if you don't!

How to remain calm... Don't go if you can't!

How to maintain your head above water… Don't go if you don't know how!

How to take care of one another… Don't go if you are unwilling!

The secret to survival, for the brave aviator in our story, is all of the above. His P.F.D. was securely on before he closed the canopy and lifted off the flat top. He knew enough not to concern himself with the largest and deepest ocean. He simply dealt with the four square feet of water around him. The initials P.F.D. stand for *personal flotation device*. Put it on! Never take your eyes off any child in your party who is in or near the water. *"We only left him alone for a second,"* is not the epitaph you want on your child's grave marker.

Tigger

SCENE TWENTY-TWO

Mike

• • • • • • •

Cody was a nine-year-old cowboy. If his second-best friend was his rope, then his first best friend was his dog Mike. He liked the dog because he was all companion and no talk. After the worst day at school and it was most of them, the sight of that dog running toward him in the afternoon sun, was all he needed to take the hurt out of a very misunderstood day.

Mike's real name was San Miguel, the Shepherd. He was named for the California mission near the place where he was born. He was an Australian Shepherd. On one end, as that fine breed does, he had one brown eye and one blue eye and on the other, he had the tiniest stub of a tail you've ever seen. In between, he had a heart of gold and a wonderful soft and curly coat of black and white fur, with caramel poured on top and drizzled down the sides. Bounding along on the dusty road, in the morning light, he looked as much like a fancy dessert, as he did a faithful cow dog. Before he came to be Cody's companion, he had served on a ranch, working cattle.

Mike was loyal. He didn't need the piece of rope the boy had tied onto his collar, but Cody had promised his mom that outside of his yard, he would always use a leash. Mike would never have left his master's side.

Tigger

See photo of Mike on my website:
www.dougcoxonline.com/mind-movies-photos

SCENE TWENTY-THREE

Lerno

● ● ● ● ● ● ●

I recently used this word onstage during a seminar. It is a word that I made up, encompassing the differences between learning and knowing. I spoke and then watched my wonderful audience try to process what they had heard. Old friends and clients just sat back and said to themselves, in silence, what is Cox up to now. A handful of newbies asked in silence *"what the hell is a Lerno?"* The rest were the target of my tickle.

I have always been the one to say, proudly, oh-my-gosh I didn't know that. I was well into my twenties when my older brother asked me what the heck I was talking about when I said *"voy-la?"* I showed him the word in a cartoon book and he almost fell out of his chair laughing! You mean *"voila"* don't you? What might have been, for many, a moment of humiliation, was instead a moment of revelation and humor for me… Voila! *(Wah-Lah)*

The folks, who want to know everything, will forever

fall short and find themselves embarrassed. Those of us, who are hungry for new knowledge, will forever be celebrating a life of never ending discovery.

Always happily thirsty,
Tigger

SCENE TWENTY-FOUR

The Bearded Rock

● ● ● ● ● ● ●

Winter had suddenly swerved left and headed straight away into spring. The afternoon air was warm, balmy and very welcoming, as we pulled into our driveway. Outside my car I heard a mysterious humming sound and discovered that the air around me was full of bees.

As you know, from my photos and stories, I am a great fan of these honey-makers and so I was honored to find myself surrounded by a swarm of these wonderful pollinators… Walking around the car, I discovered what could only be described as a bearded rock! Our yard had been chosen as a swarm-sight and thousands of our neighbor bees had set up camp on one of our desert rocks.

My daughter is the president of the Sonoma County Beekeepers Association, so with great enthusiasm I reached out to her with the news and a request for guidance. Kelli said, before shipping them off to a local beekeeper, we should give them a day or so. She explained that they were most likely in search of a new hive-sight and once the scouts returned with the target, they would head out to their new home. So right!

Within thirty-six hours the rock sat alone again. Somewhere nearby a new honey factory was opening for business.

Please Bee My Honey…
Tigger

SCENE TWENTY-FIVE

Goldilocks

• • • • • • • •

In my book, *"SH-Boom,"* I created a whole chapter about my commitment to The Pathway... If you are a subscriber to this Desert Wind newsletter, you already know about the Pathway. Some of you have actually come to share this pilgrimage with me. So many miles, so many smiles, so many tears and so many new friends and faces.

Today, near the top, I saw a familiar face appear over the hill and through the sage brush. I was touched by the visit because I have not seen her for some months and came to believe that she was gone away for the summer or perhaps forever. When we first met, over a year ago, on the Pathway, she was shy and just a bit standoffish. As I do, with animals new to me, I simply sat down on the bench, at the top of Doug's Mountain and allowed her to decide on friendship or no. To my great joy, the answer was yes! Not knowing the facts, I named her *"Goldilocks!"* That day we began a relationship that included her appearing, usually when I least expected it, bounding like a glorious lion, out to greet me. She was a golden beauty, silhouetted against the blue southwestern sky.

I was very happy to see her today, home from 4 months in Minnesota. Her Master, Greg gently and graciously informed me that Goldilocks' real name is *"Hutch"* and *she* is definitely a *he!*

I hear that dogs are very forgiving…
Tigger

See photo of Goldilocks on my website:
www.dougcoxonline.com/mind-movies-photos

SCENE TWENTY-SIX

Holes

● ● ● ● ● ● ●

My first Levis were bought for me when I was four years old. They came from a dry goods store in Altadena, California. How I loved those indigo treasures. To this day I remember the wonderful smell of that stiff blue denim, as I pulled them out of the bag.

These were my chaps, my work uniform, my magic carpet, and my protection from poison oak, rattle snakes and bad guys. I quickly discovered that if I ran out of the house early in the morning and only returned indoors after dark, I could wear my one pair of *cowboy* pants for days on end without my mom ever catching on and hijacking them into the washing machine.

In those britches I fed chickens, rode horses, ran through the brush, swam in the creek, crawled over mountains and played incredible, glorious football games in the mud. I played hide and seek, kick the can, hid from kissy-face relatives and on golden afternoons I was Robin Hood, Roy Rogers and Geronimo, all in one day!

I remember slowly but surely watching the dark blue fade into a pale shadow of the original color and I can still celebrate the first tiny hole that appeared at my knee. This was my great adventure of the traveling pants!

Breaking News! A company has now perfected a way to eliminate that whole experience. With lasers, sand paper, machines and razors, they can edit out the complete joy of one childhood and the *hole* adventure.

Meet you in the yard!
Tigger

SCENE TWENTY-SEVEN

The Letter

● ● ● ● ● ● ● ●

In this, the week of Valentine's Day, I wanted to ask you how long it's been since you wrote a letter to a loved one? *"My baby, she wrote me a letter..."* Fifty years ago when the *Box Tops* recorded those words in a studio in Memphis, Tennessee, they had no intention of encouraging written correspondence but that's exactly what they accomplished.

My dad, Charlie Cox, whom I adored, used to carry in his briefcase, cards, writing paper, envelopes and stamps. On his business trips he would jot a note of affection or information and drop it in the post, to share with his distant family and friends. How I loved opening the mail box to discover those communiques! The Box Tops song reminded me!

In Jim Henson's film, *The Dark Crystal,* Kira, the female child of the two surviving Gelflings explains to Jen, the male, that writing is *words that stay.* Charlie Brown, as I called my dad, has been dead for many years now but I still enjoy opening that folder of those wonderful encouraging words, written in his beautiful cursive hand so very many years ago. Kira reminded me.

For those who have eyes and ears, the world around us is forever revealing hints, nudges and secrets. It is we who may choose to heed or discard these whispers.

How about a note of love and appreciation set down in your own hand, to share with one that you love… It may just last throughout the ages.

Tigger

SCENE TWENTY-EIGHT

Beyove

• • • • • • •

At four years of age our youngest son came to join us, from Memphis Tennessee. From a downtown apartment, his whole life was moving to a small farmhouse on a windswept hillside in Santa Barbara California; quite a cultural shock. As this tousled headed young fellow's new father, I wanted to make sure that his first night, his initial moments in a strange place, were comforting as opposed to terrifying.

As the sun began to set, I offered to introduce him to some new friends. With a puzzled look he examined the empty hillside and asked where? Together, beneath the darkening sky, I tucked him deep into his brand new sleeping bag. Lying back on the ground I urged him to help me find the first star. *"There it is!"* He exclaimed, so excited to make the first discovery. *"I see one too,"* I shared. *"There one is,"* he shouted. I didn't see it so I asked him to show me where. Pointing toward the sky he exclaimed, *"There it is, right beyove the other one!"* *"Did you mean above"*

I asked? *"No"* he said, "beyove." "Perhaps you mean beyond" I ventured. *"No,"* he said very definitely *"it's right beyove the other one."* And that's when I knew that the word was exactly right. By the time we had counted to ten our little man was sound asleep.

As I carried him inside and tucked him into his brand new bunk bed he had ten new celestial friends to keep him company on his first night of a wonderful new life… Do you think that the wise men ever looked up and wondered what the star *beyove* them would come to mean.

Happy, blessed days,
Tigger

SCENE TWENTY-NINE

Sunshine

● ● ● ● ● ● ●

My friend, John Denver, sang *"Sunshine on my shoulders makes me happy…"* And in his wisdom continued on to sing, *"Sunshine in my eyes can make me cry…"* All living things, on this third stone from the sun, require sunlight to be born, to grow and to flourish. It is also important for us to remember, that it is under that same sun that we pass from this life.

Our sadness is, like our happiness, very real and needs to be given voice and therefore brought to life. It is my intention, going forward, to find as many moments of sunlight that I can find. In that light, I will laugh and cry and dance with everything inside me. I will find no time to belittle or degrade those with whom I share this life. I will remember that there is a clear difference between being tough and being mean and whatever others may choose to say or do, I will, to the best of my ability and discipline, stand, walk, ride, speak and live my time in toughness and joy.

"We are but a moment's sunlight, fading in the grass…"
(Jesse Colin Young)

My dream is… To make the most of my sunlight!
Tigger

SCENE THIRTY

A Blessing

● ● ● ● ● ● ●

They stood on the threshold between the world of man and the mighty jungle. The young girl wanted desperately to cross over and enter that deep, mysterious green place. More than anything she wanted to meet the wolves. The boy-wolf, Mowgli, stood beside her. Who could be a better guide? He stopped just short of the jungle apron and raised his voice in the way of Akela, his adopted father wolf… and he sang. As his call echoed through the tangle before them, he stood silently and listened. The breeze above them whispered in the Bodhi, Sandalwood and Banana trees. Then at last, he translated what he had heard, *"wood and water, wind and tree, jungle favour, go with thee… We may enter the jungle safely now,"* he said, and off they ran.

I have always been happier outdoors than I have been within. I believe one reason may be that I am so connected to nature. I am a wild man. Perhaps it was reading, as a young boy, the writings of Rudyard

Kipling or the stories of Mark Twain, Robert Louis Stevenson and Jack London, that inspired me to pause before venturing into the mountains, the big city, the sea or the jungle, to ask a silent blessing on my adventures.

Each day, just before I head up Doug's Mountain, I give thanks for my journey and each day I am granted not only safe passage but clear eyes to see, fresh ears to hear and an open mind to receive the wonders of this magnificent desert world of ours.

Come away with me…
Tigger

SCENE THIRTY-ONE

Forsaken

• • • • • • • •

"How can anyone live in this God forsaken place?"
Flying in or flying out of Las Vegas, I have heard these
words so many times... Such thoughts and expressions
can only spring from a self-imposed blindness and
ignorance to the earth's truth. People live all
over the world and in a thousand different climates,
locations and situations, but most of us can and
have found a redeeming comfort in our surroundings
and residence.

For me the desert has become my refuge, my monastery,
my companion. Far from God forsaken, I find, in the
deep silence of the southwest, the sweetest meditative
invitation and the most divine, receptive ear for my
prayers and gratitude.

If you will examine, as I do, the beauty of a cactus
blossom, you will find in the artwork, from the
Master's Hand, the makings of the world's greatest
cathedral. For those who have eyes, this place is

just one of the many heavens on earth!

Thank you for sharing,
Tigger

SCENE THIRTY-TWO

Spanking

● ● ● ● ● ● ●

I never did spank my kids. We are just not a spanking kind of family. That is not to say that I was not strict or stern with my children. I am just a firm hand on a gentle rein kind of cowboy and it seems to have worked out quite well. I simply tried to listen- to and understand the young person in front of me. I believe that part of the success was that I was a dad first and a friend second.

In my opinion, my kids are simply the best in the world and so today, I have the great joy of being friends with my offspring and they are, more and more frequently becoming my teachers and mentors. (Please don't tell them about this, as things could get sticky.)

If we are going to be the last generation on the planet to honor the simple virtues of courtesy, kindness, caring and respect, we need to step up into our leadership role. We cannot, in good conscience, blame the generations that are so lost in their technology, that they cannot look into one another's eyes and speak in whole sentences. I think we need to begin spanking their parents immediately.

OMG,
Tigger

SCENE THIRTY-THREE

Sabor A Mi

• • • • • • • •

Randi and Hector are very dear friends of many years. They were coming to share dinner in our home. I asked if Hector would like to invite his elderly mom and dad to join us. He replied, "That would be great!" We shared a wonderful dinner and a glass of wine and then it came to me that although we had talked all the way through our meal, we spoke only English. Hector's quiet mom and dad spoke only Spanish. I excused myself and changed the dinner music to a CD I have loved since I was a child. Trio Los Ponchos, singing, *"The Romantic music of Mexico."*

As the songs began to play, a new and beautiful voice came to join in and we were astounded. Hector's mother was singing along, as if she had been a lead singer who had never left the group. *"Me Voy Pal Pueblo,"* *"Piel Canela,"* *"Sabor A Mi,"* she knew them all. What an evening. Although Hector's Mother and Father are no longer with us, his father's soft spoken voice, in perfect Spanish and the voice of his Angel, still fill our memories, our hearts and our home.

Where does one find enchantment these days? Perhaps in the presence of strangers and elders and the willingness to be still, experience and be enchanted.

Muchas Gracias Amigos,
Tigger

SCENE THIRTY-FOUR

Patterns

• • • • • • • •

I have never been good at math! I found, over the years, that if a teacher could spark my interest, or help me find a connection, I could become a top student; well, better late than never. I recently saw a PBS special that knocked me into the world of mathematics forever. NOVA, *"The Great Math Mystery,"* is the event.

As most of my readers know, I have been photographing flowers and their creatures for many years. Until experiencing this program, I had never considered the obvious patterns that exist in the wonderful world of flora. The fun begins with my awakening to the "Fibonacci" (Pronounced: fib-o-na-chee) sequence in nature. The seed pattern in a sunflower, the spiral in a nautilus shell and the curve of a wave, are common examples of the equation that occurs so often in nature. From the whirlpool of a galaxy, to the swirl in my flower photos, you can see Fibonacci's *"Golden Spiral."* Einstein loved this!

Although I am sure that I will never thoroughly understand it, there is a mathematical formula that celebrates this glorious phenomenon.

I am a faithful student now,
Tigger

SCENE THIRTY-FIVE

Chip

● ● ● ● ● ● ● ●

When the desert wind blows heavy in the late spring, from time to time it picks up trash, particularly light grocery bags and deposits them in our wild and beautiful monastery. This morning on our way up Doug's Mountain, my oldest son Dave, stopped us mid-hike and said, *"I'll be right back dad!"*

He walked off into the sage brush about fifty yards and when he returned I understood why. He had gone off to retrieve a piece of trash that had blown into our beloved desert.

It was a joy to see this fine young man doing what so many fail to do.

See what others don't see!

Do what others won't do!

And recognize the power in the smallest of good deeds!

I am very proud to be a chip off his young block!
Tigger

SCENE THIRTY-SIX

Savage Beasts

● ● ● ● ● ● ● ●

I just watched a hundredth re-running of the fine and funny film, *"Young Frankenstein?"* Remember?

My Uncle Rowan was an actor. He appeared on Walt Disney's Wonderful World of Color, in films like, *"The Secret of Old Glory Mine,"* and *"Inky the Crow..."* He was an irascible rascal, with much and varied talent but a grumpy demeanor that frightened us kids.

Once we visited his Silver Fox Farm, in the Big Bear Mountains of Southern California. After a long ride up the mountain and a busy day at playing cowboys, us young'uns were wound up tighter than a tick. Tucked into our sleeping bags in the little back room of the farm house, the six of us found it hard to sleep and so we got the giggles and stirred up quite a ruckus! Suddenly, from the front of the little wood frame home, drifted the sound of the sweetest music. The beautiful notes of Uncle Rowan's violin filled our little room and surrounded us. Before long, try though we might, we were out like a light. It seems that the strains of Londonderry Air, or *"Danny Boy"* as we know it, played by my grumpy but talented uncle, were too much, even for little cowboys and girls.

Perhaps the best way to tame the savage beast or overthrow a government, would be with force and violins!

Tigger

SCENE THIRTY-SEVEN

Coming About

● ● ● ● ● ● ●

The wind is cool and fresh. Blowing in beneath the Golden Gate Bridge, it tastes of salt and faraway times and places. The Sagittarius is riding smoothly and nicely, making way, as we hold our course toward Ayala Cove. The fog dances, as it moves and dissipates across the face of San Francisco Bay. It is one of many Memorial Days spent with my beloved friend, Jim. He is a Navy veteran and as we head out, on this special day of remembrance, between the long silences, we talk softly about our appreciation for heroes and sheroes, both living and dead.

Once around Angel Island and into Raccoon Strait, with the mighty Pacific Ocean ahead, we bring her into the wind and prepare to come about for home. The main sheet snaps to attention and our conversation shifts to family and friends, the living and the loved.

Perhaps, this one Memorial Day we might all do well to connect with those we hold dear, overcome our reserve and simply say, *"I Love You!"*

I do love you…
Tigger

See our photo on my website:
www.dougcoxonline.com/mind-movies-photos

SCENE THIRTY-EIGHT

Lawman

• • • • • • • •

Many years ago, when I was a young man in the firearms business, a customer came into our gun store in Pasadena, California. As he strode through the main door, I said, *"Howdy, how may I serve you today?"* He said he wanted to buy what he called a *"Six-Gun!"* When I asked his purpose for the handgun, he replied, *"I am an actor and I am preparing for a role in a Disney movie."* He seemed very excited that an actor, trained in New York, had gotten his first important role in a western series entitled, *"The Nine Lives of El Fago Baca..."*

I not only found a fine used Colt 45, but I was asked to modify the weapon so that the action would be smoother and faster in the many uses of a lawman from old New Mexico. This was the first of my meetings and opportunities to serve, Salvatore "Robert" Loggia, who added his magnificent talents and characters to such films as, An Officer and a Gentleman, Prizzi's Honor, Scarface and The Jagged Edge, the role for which he received a Best Supporting Actor nomination. You will remember his wonderful face and character creation... I will always remember the kind and courteous gentleman, for whom I once helped create a very fast *"six gun."*

Always a Cowboy,
Tigger

SCENE THIRTY-NINE

Chance

• • • • • • •

In the movie *Rio Bravo*, starring John Wayne, Dean Martin, Angie Dickinson and Walter Brennan, the character, played by the Duke, was named *"Chance!"* The word always makes me stop and think about the number of people who have given me a chance; a simple priceless opportunity, to join a team, to sing in the choir, to dance as a clumsy teenager in the high school gym. We all have this wonderful ego that loves to say, *"Hey! I make my own chances. I earned this opportunity. Nobody ever gave me anything."* In every case, to some degree this is true but when I think back across this wonderful life of mine, I remember the chances and my heart fills with gratitude!

From my first job, throwing newspapers, to my opportunity at age 14 working at a service station and at last, the chance to travel the world inspiring *"perfect"* strangers, these were the breaks granted to me by people of business who liked my cut and trusted me enough to take a chance on this skinny kid. Today, I still remember the names of every boss I ever had. In my thanks, prayers and meditation every evening, I whisper each name.

For you see, without that *"chance"* and all of the chances you've been given, we wouldn't be sharing this story right now.

Thanks for the chance,
Tigger

SCENE FORTY

Seeing

• • • • • • • •

I love the Camelot Fable... From the first time I read, *"The Once and Future King,"* I was fascinated by the romance and mystery of the story. I was touched by Arthur's Commitment to the sword, Excalibur and his promise to use, *"might for right!"* But mostly, as a child, I loved the magic and the mystery of Merlin. He taught me that Wizards can *"remember forward"* and so... See into the future!

Seven days before the tragic events in Orlando, I selected a photo for my Friday Flowers to share with my friends. As I always do, I said a prayer and then set my mind on the choice of words to accompany the magic of the Master's Hand on this flower photo and the creature nestled or hiding within. The title that came to me was, *"Red Flowers... On an Ambush!"*

My photos are sent out on Thursday evening, to be in your Friday email. From my room in the Seminole Hard Rock, in Hollywood Florida, I opened my travel laptop to discover that it was blue —screen frozen. I could not send out my email. From my room in Hollywood, Florida, I first heard about the incredible tragedy in Orlando. By the time I returned to my office in Las Vegas, I was astounded at the choice of the title of my photo.

It is not enough to *wish* that such tragedies would not occur; we must act in love and respect for all humanity, to make this wish a reality.

Let the world be a better place and let it begin with me...

Tigger

SCENE FORTY-ONE

Wonder

• • • • • • •

As another incredible winter draws to a close, I have an idea. This spring and summer, why not go somewhere new and wonderful? When I was eighteen years old I bought my first Golden Eagle Passport to our National Park System. I have purchased one every year since, until I earned a permanent one at age sixty-two.

The greatest education we can ever hope to gain is to experience new visions, fresh vistas and the flavor of a new world. If you have not looked up at El Capitan, in Yosemite National Park in winter, you have missed it. If you have not walked the battlefield at Lexington, or stood in silence where the shot heard 'round the world was fired, you have missed it. If you have not wandered in the rain beneath the fragrant Giant Redwoods or stood in reverence at the feet of Lady Liberty, you have missed it. To leap from the top of Two Medicine falls, in Glacier National Park or dip beneath the cool, blue pacific, at the Channel Islands or dance with wolves in Yellowstone, is to touch the magic.

Wherever life finds you now, there is a park, pool, nature center, museum or a zoo waiting for your arrival. Simon and Garfunkel sang: *"But you can take a crosstown bus if it's raining or it's cold and the animals will love it if you do!"* A visit to someplace you have never been, is the difference between knowing and not knowing. I am in New Jersey and Pennsylvania, visiting my old friends George Washington and Paul Revere. For me this is the doorway to my doctorate of Lifeology! Open Sesame… See you out there…

Ranger Tigger

SCENE FORTY-TWO

Thump

● ● ● ● ● ● ●

By the time we got to him, he was quivering on the ground beneath our kitchen window. The *Horned Lark,* common to Southern Nevada, had flown, full speed into the glass and knocked himself silly. Before we ever touch a wild creature, we run through our checklist: Is it a juvenile; is it in a place where, left alone it might recover and most importantly, is it able to fly? The answer to all was negative, so, after speaking softly, for a few moments, I very carefully and gently held my finger beneath his chest and encouraged him to hop up on my hand. He pondered the risk and then stepped gingerly onto a friendly hand.

I wish that I had a heroic rescue story to share but I simply held him, motionless for about 15 minutes and he finally began to recover his senses and survey his surroundings. At last he was able to turn his head and shift his position on my hand.

Finally, he gave us an over the shoulder glance to

say thanks and then flew off into the springtime desert of our monastery.

Life is precious and the opportunity to observe it up close and personal is a treasure of moments. You can do it too...

Tigger

SCENE FORTY-THREE

Valiant

● ● ● ● ● ● ● ●

I love language… How about you? My parents and my older brother all spoke so beautifully, that dinner, around the table in the Cox house, was a grammar tutorial. We were encouraged to speak beautifully, gracefully and powerfully!

We used words that stirred the heart, mind and imagination. Lionheart, courageous, brave and selfless, are just a few of the words that describe one of my favorites, *valiant.* It is something I have always wanted to be…

At a time when language has fallen on hard times and descriptive words are being reduced to initials, perhaps we could be the ones who ride into battle armed with words of power, emblazoned across our shields and rampant on the banners above our heads.

We Ride Together…

I would love to hear your *"Power"* word!
Sir Tigger

SCENE FORTY-FOUR

Mirror

● ● ● ● ● ● ● ●

We go through our whole lives as strangers to ourselves!

Whenever I read about the untimely demise of people, either famous or infamous, I ask myself, why such a tragic ending? What are these treasured young lives looking at in the mirror and more importantly what are they seeing? When we lost Glee star, Cory Montieth, with good looks, money, fame, a family and a lovely co-star and girlfriend, I always ask myself what could possibly have led to such a conclusion. I think perhaps the answer lies not in the ending, splashed across the television and the tabloids but in the beginning of the story. Whether it is in our work/service, our relationships, our art, or our creations, our belief in ourselves determines the outcome.

There are no *"Bad Times"* only learning times. In this life, recognizing how truly important, significant and wonderful we are, will always lead to the most positive outcomes. Time for a new friend... Yourself!

Get up, get going and in all of our endeavors, let us make beautiful beginnings over and over again!

Tigger

SCENE FORTY-FIVE

Buena Vista

• • • • • • • •

Summer is on its way to the beautiful Sierra Nevada Mountains of California. High above the redwood forest, is a mountain peak known as Buena Vista. The name means *"beautiful view"* in Spanish. It is an appropriate name, for once on top, you can truly see forever.

"Dad, come quick!" my six-year-old son called out. I followed his voice around a large manzanita bush and found him crouching in front of a huge boulder. He was staring at, what I was sure would turn out to be, a bug or a snake. *"What is it?"* I asked. *"Look dad,"* he said. *"It's a tiny flower growing right out of this rock."* He paused, and then with that childlike sense of wonder, he said, *"its magic."*

That the fragrant summer wind had lifted one small seed and carried it to the top of a great mountain, was magic enough but to realize that the seed had found a crevice, sufficient earth and moisture to put down roots and rise up through the stone, was indeed a miracle.

Hold on tight to your ideas. The view from an idea, in the mind of a believer, is indeed *Una Buena Vista!*

I Believe…
Tigger

SCENE FORTY-SIX

Daylight

● ● ● ● ● ● ● ●

Just imagine… You have a seven year old child that loves to travel. He knows that Three-Hundred miles north of his home, in Altadena, California, there is a place that he loves. This destination is affectionately known as *"The Ranch."*

As a parent, there is nothing that you would rather do, than drop everything and escort your young Cowboy toward San Francisco but at this time, you simply can't. What do you do? You contact the Southern Pacific Railroad, fill out the papers, purchase the ticket and put your seven year old son, alone, on the train with a letter of instructions for the Chief-Conductor. With a hug, you wave him off on the adventure of a young lifetime.

The train that will carry him, as it did his brother before him, is called The Daylight Limited. It is a sleek ray of sunlight, that pulls out of the Glendale station in Southern California and rolls north along the most beautiful coastline in the world.

In his carry-on bag, the young traveler has a series of surprise gifts marked for opening, one each hour of the journey, to keep him more than occupied for ten glorious hours. Come lunch time, he will be personally escorted to the dining car, where he will join three adult fellow travelers and be served a marvelous luncheon in the company of these immaculately dressed passengers. Linen napkins, fine silver and beautiful china are a part of his experience.

Just as the sun begins to set, the chief comes to escort the young traveler onto the platform, where, in loving arms, he will be whisked away to Los Altos Hills and *"The Ranch"* that he loves so dearly… It was a wonderful world into which I was born. Much has changed but not the memories! Booooooooooard!

Tigger

SCENE FORTY-SEVEN

Expressions

• • • • • • • •

Do you love expressions as much as I do? I want to know what they mean, where they came from and how we might bring them back into our current conversation. Fiddlesticks you say? Poppycock, falderal, hooey, hype, hyperbole, jive, nonsense, gibberish, malarkey, balderdash, blather, drivel, piffle and plain old tomfoolery!

Could all of these marvelous words be lost from our dialogue or is it merely a coinkydink? A penny for your thoughts… Perhaps I am barking up the wrong tree but I see no reason for beating around the bush. I think that we hit the nail on the head with this one. You know that you can't judge a book by its cover but a picture paints a thousand words and when you hear it straight from the horse's mouth, you must take it with a grain of salt. It's a piece of cake!

Hey! Don't shoot me, I'm only the messenger!
Tigger

SCENE FORTY-EIGHT

Heartland

● ● ● ● ● ● ●

"Toto… I have a feeling that we're not in Kansas anymore!" Sorry Dorothy, but I am in Kansas and I couldn't be happier! I love this place… I love the farmland that stretches as far as the eye can see. I love the fields, the sky, the warm south wind, the Pretty Prairie Rodeo, the restaurants, the shopping and the history. I even love the weather, which can be as still as a sleeping kitten and turn as violent as a volcano. But most of all, I love the people!

This is a place where making friends with one generation is a sure sign that you will be friends with the next three. Where a handshake is as good as a contract and a person's word is all that you need to strike a bargain. Kansas is an invitation to visit the best of America and leave as an even better American. Time definitely changes things.

The call sign for this airport where I landed today, is MCI. It once stood for Mid-Continent International

Airport, a perfect name for a place where barnstormers and pioneers of the sky, once dropped down from the heavens and onto one tiny single runway. Today, Dreamliner's and a hundred sleek, silver aircraft, bring millions of international passengers to Kansas City International Airport. My wish is that they slow down just enough to realize that they have disembarked in the *Heartland* of the greatest country the world has ever known!

Thanks for having me,
Tigger

SCENE FORTY-NINE

High

• • • • • • • •

The beverages are ice cold… The afternoon breeze is easy and smells of juniper and pine. As the golden sun is disappearing behind the great mountains, the deer are slipping out of their napping place in the oaks and walking warily down the slope through the wax current, chokecherry and willow. Our conversation is low and sparse. Silence is the keynote. The punctuation is provided by a steller's jay in the tree close at hand and the red tail hawk in the blue sky high above.

CUE THE MUSIC

John Denver, *"Rocky Mountain High."*

ROLL CAMERAS

ENTER ROBERT REDFORD ON HORSEBACK...

Is it a film shoot? Nope! It's an afternoon on my son's deck in the Rocky Mountains. The only thing missing is my daughter but the excited barking of Tank, their dog, tells me that she will be here momentarily.

Want to join us? Put in your ear buds and download *"Summer Rain,"* by Johnny Rivers or *"Colorado,"* by The Flying Burrito Brothers or *"Rocky Mountain Christmas,"* by the Nitty Gritty Dirt Band!

In memory of those who offered the ultimate sacrifice! Tigger, Chris and Janie

SCENE FIFTY

Lost and Found

• • • • • • • •

I am a dyed in the wool Disney fan… From Marceline to Mickey Mouse, I love the journey. When Disney opened their California Adventure, in 2001, I was lucky enough to be invited with the press, for the media opening. We were first taken to *"Soarin' over California,"* a simulated hang glider ride, which took us from Malibu, at dusk, up over the Golden Gate Bridge, and into wine country, orange orchards and Yosemite National Park. As it is with Disney, the cinematography was absolutely breathtaking and the experience was enhanced by Smell-O-Vision. During our flight, we could smell the surf, the orange blossoms and the vineyards below. If you have not, you must see and experience *"Soarin'…"*

The second venue, to which we were introduced, was titled Golden Dreams. It was a beautiful visual history of the early days of California. It was a stand up, lean against a railing, 360 degree history lesson, led by Califia, the mythical Queen of California, with a voiceover by Whoopi Goldberg. She was a terrific narrator and guide and in the darkened theatre made a touching, humorous presentation of California's birth and early days. What I remember most about the now closed attraction, was something that the geniuses at Disney did to end the stirring production. As the theme music came to its crescendo, the lights began to rise and we prepared to exit the theater, Queen Califia, in her regular Whoopi Goldberg voice yelled out *"Hey Lady… You forgot your purse!"* Naturally all of us, women, men and kids alike, checked around our feet and surroundings for our belongings. One phrase, properly spoken, eliminated millions of dollars in lost and found challenges. Disney Smart!

The theme song, *"Just One Dream,"* from the now lost adventure, still brings goose pimples and tears.

Meet you in The Magic Kingdom…
Tigger

SCENE FIFTY-ONE

Cinco De Mayo

● ● ● ● ● ● ●

Crossing busy Alameda Street, from the beautifully restored Union Train Station in Los Angeles, California, you are headed straight into another world. Olvera Street is the oldest part of the City of Angels. On Cinco de Mayo, it is a festival of fragrance, color, sound and motion. Everywhere around me Spanish is spoken. It is a beautiful dancing language and properly expressed it connects us to a much larger world.

I practice by doing my own phonetic version of the words: Hola, (hello) pronounced *"O-La…"* Cinco de Mayo (Fifth of May) is pronounced *"Seenco-Day-My-Yo…"* When I was born in Southern California, our Mexican friends taught me to play my little guitar and sing my very first song; *"Me Boy Pal Pueblo,"* (Going to town).

As a very young boy, I discovered that properly pronouncing the words of a language, other than my own, helped me to develop my intellect in three very specific ways. First, by learning a few simple words in a new language, I was expanding my vocabulary. Second, I learned that by properly pronouncing the words and phrases, I was beginning to understand the culture of the people as well. And finally, I found that by working hard to pronounce the words properly, I was demonstrating respect for not only the language but the people with whom I was speaking. More than once, since then, I have, based on my respect for the culture of others, been asked to help them speak English more beautifully!

Mmmm! I love the smell of hand patted tortillas and Mexican spices on the warm afternoon breeze. My heart beats faster when I hear la musica drifting across the courtyard from Los Mariachis, as they play *"Sabor A Mi."* The flashing colors of the dancers as they whirl to the beat of Old Mexico, move my spirit to dance. I must also admit that an ice-cold margarita, served at La Golondrina restaurant, is a perfect ending to a Southern California adventure...

Muchas Gracias,
Tigger

SCENE FIFTY-TWO

Holly

• • • • • • • •

She only came for a visit… Our wonderful neighbors were truly pet sitting for a matter of weeks. We found out that she was a *"res"* dog; a blessed rescue.

Out on the trails and up to the summit of Doug's Mountain, she either led or followed Chantal for hours on end. She was sweet and courteous to all who met her on the trails but at home it was a different story. One day a repairman came to fulfill his duties in our neighbor's home. He wore a uniform with a badge and something about his presence set the beautiful Holly into a frenzy.

When I heard the story, I was touched by the fact that someone, somewhere in her history, a male human mistreated such a sweet dog to the point that she was terrified by this innocent workman's presence. How can it be that anyone of us human beings could treat a fellow creature so badly that they would react to us in such a way? Sadly there are those among us who do the same with children and the results are often disastrous.

Holly: a decorative branch and berry for the holidays. Holly: One half of a Neil Diamond song title. Holly: a sweet caramel coloured friend and companion to those of us who offer her the same…

Thanks for sharing,
Tigger

*See photo of Holly on my website:
www.dougcoxonline.com/mind-movies-photos*

SCENE FIFTY-THREE

The Fox

●　●　●　●　●　●　●　●

The afternoon wind was fresh and cold, as we walked across the snowy parking lot. Incline Village at Lake Tahoe is magic at Christmastime! The sun sends showers of light through the beautiful tall trees, the lake is cobalt blue and the air smells like December. For me, the only thing better than outside, is *inside,* with dear and precious friends.

The doorway to the beautiful salon, swings open to reveal a truly bright, classy and professional place of beauty and business. The faces of the two people that run to greet us, are wonderfully familiar and welcoming. The first time that I saw these bright shining countenances, was from the stage, at Rickey's Hyatt House, in Palo Alto California. I had come to inspire and they had come to learn. They were the kind of people you dream of, being in the front row of your program. Over the years, as it turned out, I learned far more from them than they learned from me.

Life and ALOHA took them away from the Sierra Nevada Mountains and the trade-winds carried them to the island of Maui, in Hawaii. The latest lesson came in the form of a post on Facebook, which informed us that Ted *"The Fox"* had passed away in his sleep. They are and will always be, two of the brightest lights in the firmament. My lesson... How lucky I was to have always taken the moment to hug these two human treasures. I love you, Ted and Susan Fox and I love my friends throughout the world. If I have not told you, please forgive me...

Aloha: Until we meet again,
Tigger

SCENE FIFTY-FOUR

A Summer Place

• • • • • • • •

I know, it's only spring, but for us, it is time once again for our annual trek to California. On the south end of Carmel Beach sits the beautiful Walker Residence, a Frank Lloyd Wright home, that was used in the final scenes of the romantic film, *A Summer Place.* Those who don't know the movie, certainly will remember the haunting theme song.

Each year, both family and friends, join us to celebrate the life and passing of our daughter Barbee and our grandson Danny. As both of these bright lights lived, laughing, playing and celebrating, we will be living up to their legacy and having a wonderful time, in one of the most beautiful places on earth, Carmel-By-The-Sea! If only we all had eyes to see, we would realize that every life, every family, every story, whatever its size, is a story worth telling, a song worth singing and a movie worth making.

We find our joy by treasuring fond memories, looking

with hope to the future and living each moment to the fullest.

See you on the beach…
Tigger

SCENE FIFTY-FIVE

Wings One

• • • • • • •

I have passed beneath this wonderful huge tree nearly once a day for the last three years. Beneath these majestic branches, I've heard the song of mockingbirds, shrike, quail, great horned owls, mourning doves and the inspiring chip-chip-chip of the lightning fast sparrow hawk. This morning brought a wondrous surprise. As I approached the tree, I perceived what I thought was the wind, whispering through the leaves. The sound came not from one branch but from the whole tree. It was as if an orchestra of wood nymphs struck up a sweet and wonderful chorus, just for me.

However, a quick glance up made it quite clear that there was not a breath of wind this day. As I took my place beneath this verdant treasure, I realized that what I was hearing was the joyful sound of a million tiny wings. The spring celebration of sap production was upon us and the bees had come to celebrate, dance and dine.

A million wings, at two per bee, means that the tree was sharing its branches, leaves and sustenance with half-a-million miracle workers.

Honey I'm home!
Tigger

SCENE FIFTY-SIX

Who

• • • • • • • •

It is a soft, rare, rainy day in the desert of the southwest. The perfume of sage, greasewood, cactus and thirsty moist earth, fills the air. I love climbing my mountain every day and I count rainy days as very special. In the clouds above me, as I climb *"up,"* I hear a Boeing 737 climbing *"out."* Ten-thousand feet up there, out of sight, that beautiful silver bird is heading eastbound with a load of wonderful passengers.

I can't see them but I know that they are wonderful. I can't see if they are heading home or leaving home. I can't see their skin color, or how and where they worship. I can't see how they love or who they love, I simply know that they do. I cannot see their politics or how they voted. I can't see if they are leaving my city richer or poorer, for their time on *"The Strip."* Having flown millions of miles myself, I care for their safety and wellbeing, so I always whisper a silent prayer: *"Travel safely, silver-bird and God*

Speed my sisters and brothers. Amen."

From my earthbound monastery, I can only imagine who is up there and how wonderful they might be!

Bon Voyage,
Tigger

SCENE FIFTY-SEVEN

Holiday Parking

● ● ● ● ● ● ● ●

Have you ever noticed how much you can tell about folks by simply watching them? Perhaps our family gets the award for being the most observant team of all, particularly my CSI kids. Whether it is in California, Colorado or Nevada, they never seem to miss a trick. We recently shared a discussion about people and holiday parking and this is what I learned! If you are in a parking lot, waiting for your wife to finish her shopping, it's like watching a CW sitcom. When the driver, any age, any gender, comes into view, barreling into the driveway, they believe that the entry speed determines what comes next. The NASCAR freak always bounces over the sidewalk, tears out the undercarriage of their already dented vehicle and zips into the spot at an angle that makes exit and entry virtually impossible. They then climb up and out of their overheated buggy like a trapped anaconda.

The slow pokes, or as my kids call them, *"Lollygaggers,"* always wander around the parking lot like forlorn gold miners searching for the lost mother lode. Once located, and this could take four or five laps around the track, they finally need three tries just to enter the chosen spot. By the time they nurse their ore cart into the mine entry, you can be sure their vehicle will end up straight away, but so far to one side you could hold a rodeo on that side and need a shoe horn to exit on the other.

Then there is the BMW fighter pilot who whips into the parking lot and without running over a bag boy or frightening an elderly couple, assesses the target area, chooses the bogey, presses the bomb release and shoots it squarely into the spot. The best part of our discussion begins when one of us asks the $64,000 question: Who in the world taught these people to drive? Well… What do you think?

Tigger

SCENE FIFTY-EIGHT

Nails

● ● ● ● ● ● ● ●

Autumn in the southwestern United States is a wonder. The temperature is down from the summer scorch and the sky is azure blue, with a whisper of clouds sent our way by the Pacific Ocean. Starting up my trail, I see heading down toward me, a young family; a fine looking mom and dad, with a sweet little child leading the way. I admired the parents immediately for allowing the four-year-old to feel her independence, without them clutching and grabbing at her every inch of the way.

Once face to face, we exchanged greetings, the little one holding out her hand to me. I may be a rodeo cowboy but I can still spot fresh nail polish when I see it! *"Not only a very good hiker, but a fine young lady I see…What beautiful nails you have!"*

She beamed up at me and held both hands up for a further inspection. She nailed it!

And a little child shall lead us!

God Bless the child. God Bless America!
Tigger

SCENE FIFTY-NINE

All the Way

● ● ● ● ● ● ● ●

Have you ever really shared a sleigh ride? I'm sure that many of my readers have not ever had the pleasure. It is everything you imagined and everything (and more) that is promised in Leroy Anderson's recording of *"Sleigh Ride!"* It is cozy beneath the lap blankets and warm where the hot chocolate has jiggled its way onto your lap.

It is the beautiful red bird in the bare branch above, standing out against the white canvas of fresh snow. It is the smell of a pinewood fire on the crisp December air and the sound of leather traces and creaking harness in the still air. It is the runner tracks in the snow behind us and the dream of friends and family, that lie ahead but most of all; it is here… this place, this precious moment in time.

"Jingle bells, jingle bells, jingle all the way." We make of this moment, this world, what we will. At this time of year I am touched by those of us who

only allow themselves to see the northern end of two southbound horses. You are missing it! Smile, laugh, sing, hug dream and enjoy the ride!

Tigger

SCENE SIXTY

Calls

● ● ● ● ● ● ● ●

On the deck, above the shoreline, the afternoon breeze
whispers across our faces and moves on… into the
changing season. Before us, the autumn sun sinks low
across the water and dances orange and red through the
branches of the fragile trees. Basswood, elm, blue
beech, black cherry and oak, balsam fir and Norway
pine, the fragrance of changing leaves fills the air
around us. In the distance comes a call, mysterious
and haunting. The sound is both clear and stunning
and it moves closer, ever closer, until suddenly the
whisper of wings above us let us in on the secret.
The loons of Trout Lake are winging home to their
nesting place.

Henry David Thoreau wrote about this moment in his
book "Walden." Katherine Hepburn, "On Golden Pond,"
called out to these wondrous creatures. Native
people knew the language of the loons well; the four
distinct calls needed little translation; the tremolo
announcing alarm, the yodel, staking a territorial

claim, the simple hoot, sharing intimate conversations and the haunting wail that echoes across the northern lakes ensuring connection between pairs, families and praise-be… us humans.

I loved this afternoon,
Tigger

Google: Solitudes, volume twelve, "Listen to the Loons!" And share them all!

SCENE SIXTY-ONE

Lost

● ● ● ● ● ● ●

In Kenneth Graham's wonderful book, *"The Wind in the Willows,"* the water rat exhorts his new friend the mole, to stay away from the wildwood. I say go west and see Lake Wildwood, in northern California. Visiting two beloved lifetime friends in this idyllic setting, was an absolute joy. Thanks to my GPS routing, I became completely lost and it took me two hours to go one mile from the entry gate to the doorway of Paul and Susan. On my way, I saw turkeys, mule deer and skunks, oh my. I saw the beautiful clear blue water of the lake at high noon and felt the sense of the Golden Pond that calls to all of us.

For all of my adventuresome life, I have treasured the lost places where what I came for and where I was headed, was put on divine hold, just long enough for me to experience a whole new and unexpected world of wonder.

Come along with me and we shall plan an adventure,

from which we can only hope to get lost… Together!

Tigger

SCENE SIXTY-TWO

Deposits

● ● ● ● ● ● ● ●

The couple was well past middle age, when they walked up to the bank and into the manager's office. After an exchange of pleasantries, the manager asked the long-term customers, *"How may I assist you today?"* The lady responded that as their days were passing and as they all knew, numbered, the couple wanted to look into their safe deposit box to see what was there after all of the years. The banker obliged, led the way, and pulled out the long unopened box. As bankers do, the manager stepped back graciously to allow the customers a private look into their collected goods. As the lid came open, the couple was stunned at what they saw. The box was full of garbage! *"Wha-wha-what is this?"* the lady stammered. The banker replied gently, *"Only what you have collected and deposited throughout the years…"*

"How could it be," she asked? There was a long silence and then her husband lowered his eyes and responded in the softest tone of understanding, *"We have too*

often found the worst in things instead of the best. We have remembered the worst in what happened in our life, not the best. We have seen the worst in people, not the best. It seems that perhaps we have left the gold of goodness and kindness behind and kept the garbage in our thoughts and that is what we have found in our account today."

As they left the open safety deposit box on the counter and turned to walk away, the wife took her husband's hand and with a fresh squeeze said, *"Then we shall begin again, today… I love you,"* she said softly. *"Me too,"* he replied.

Tigger

SCENE SIXTY-THREE

Ladies

• • • • • • • •

Here along the front range of the Rockies, it is that time of year, when in a matter of hours, the wind can come up warm from the south and then, as the locals cling to summer, turn upon itself and send a cold blue shock to your whole being. Autumn in the Rockies is a time of both wonder and surprises. I am here celebrating with family and friends-as-good-as-family, another year of life!

This time, along with the brush of color in the Oaks and Aspens, I also find myself surrounded by something else: flashes of orange that fill the skies and dance on the shifting winds. *"Painted Ladies,"* the wonderful butterflies, who migrate through the front-range, are all around us, from the streets of town to the runways at Denver international Airport. The autumn air is filled with these tiny treasures. Like a Disney animation, they swirl and flutter, seeming to share their fall color with everything they touch. I have been told that these wonderful little sprites are an endangered species; if this is true then this kaleidoscope of life is truly encouraging.

While October is still with us, take a walk outside and watch the flower beds around you. In most of the west, you will be treated to the wings of autumn's angels…

Tigger

SCENE SIXTY-FOUR

Run

● ● ● ● ● ● ●

I remember it best when spoken by Richard Harris, as King Arthur… *"Run boy, run!"* We had just shared my first experience of observing an eagle release. Having survived a gun shot and weeks in captivity, this magnificent symbol of courage and freedom had earned and at last won its freedom. I remember trying to capture a photo of the moment, only to find that my tears had made focusing my camera impossible.

Without a word spoken, my totem brother, Nanook and I drove from that moment of reverence, to the backside of the mountain that stands watch over the historic city of Sitka, Alaska. Still captivated by what we had witnessed, we climbed to the top of this verdant, misty mountain, to sit and contemplate the world below. My friend and guide in all things Alaskan, simply looked at me and nodded and like two schoolboys, we plunged headlong down the mountainside. Full speed over muddy ground and under tangled branches we ran, falling, laughing and stumbling until at last, muddy, bloody and grinning, we reached the bottom and the parking lot where we had left our vehicle and the world of human existence.

On our return to town, our companions looked at us and simply exclaimed, *"Where have you boys been?"* To this day I can still hear the voice of King Arthur calling out to us, in the hour of battle, *"Run boy, run!"*

And yes… I would do it again tomorrow!
Tigger

SCENE SIXTY-FIVE

Southwest

● ● ● ● ● ● ● ●

Welcome Aboard family, friends and colleagues:

I grew up with United Airlines. My first UAL flight was on a tail-dragger from Los Angeles to Lindberg Field in San Diego and one of my favorite routes is UAL#839 from LAX-Sydney Australia. I am a proud Million Mile United Flyer. In recent years I have found myself choosing more and more often, to fly a competitor. What has changed? It is simple, Southwest Airlines goes where I need to go and the fares are more reasonable. I also enjoy the courtesy and humor of the SWA crews. In short, flying is fun on Southwest.

Southwest has recently upgraded their logo. In their introductory commercial, they showed a video of the aircraft in its shiny new livery, surrounded by Team Members in uniform. It was the dialogue chosen for the voiceover, that caught my attention. As the camera pulled back from the sleek, freshly painted 737, the announcer said, *"Without the people, this is just a machine!"*

Ever lost a customer or guest? Business is not just business, it is people too! Whatever the size of your company, make sure you are going where your passengers want to go and be sure to make it fun along the way.

Is your heart still in it? Mine is!
Tigger

SCENE SIXTY-SIX

Sing

● ● ● ● ● ● ●

Every Friday, my Montana friend, Cal Fuss, emails a message of hope and joy and inspiration. They are wonderful quotes from the famous and the unknown. They are an important part of my Friday! This week he shared a quote from the Reverend Henry Van Dyke about gratitude. It was a sharp and clear wake up call for me. In our home, while I was growing up, we used to sing at the dinner table. The songs ranged from rock, Christmas, spiritual, and Songs of the Pogo to opera. I didn't say that we were good, I just said that we sang.

The Van Dyke quote reminded me of a favorite song titled, *"America for Me!"* I may have been a small country boy but the joy and inspiration that I felt when that song began was a wonder. It is a recitation by an American traveler who has headed off for Europe and then begins to appreciate and long for his home. It is the most patriotic song I have ever heard or sung. *"So it's home again, and home again, America for me! My heart is turning home again and there I long to be. In the blessed land of room enough beyond the ocean bars, where the air is full of sunlight and the flag is full of stars!"* Composed in 1909 it is both the song and the sense that we need so desperately in these conflicted times.

If you are looking not only for a reason to celebrate our great country but to share the celebration, look it up!

Henry Van Dyke (1852-1933) *"America for Me"*

It would be my honor to sing with thee!
Tigger

SCENE SIXTY-SEVEN

Hutch II

• • • • • • • •

Perhaps my Desert Wind subscribers will remember the story of *"Goldilocks,"* the golden retriever whose real name was *"Hutch."*. In this book I am including both parts of this story, because they are both important pieces of a wonderful whole. This is part two.

On my way up Doug's Mountain today, I met Greg and his wife, the owners of this sweet dog. Having missed them for a few months, I was anxious to hear the news of my golden friend. They revealed to me that Hutch was getting to an age where although he is still in good health, he can no longer make the journey up the trail. We have agreed that one day soon we will meet in the City View parking lot, at the base of the mountain, where I will be reunited with my special friend.

Life often opens the doorway of opportunity for us to consider our own future adventures. In my current radiant health, it seems a long way *down the trail,* but one day I will find myself, like Hutch, at the bottom of my beloved pathway, saying howdy and exchanging news with friends and strangers alike as they head up Doug's mountain.

For me the art and science of *positive preparation* has faithfully put me in a frame of mind that allows me, whatever the fates deliver, to go to sleep in peace and awaken each morning in joy.

Thanks Hutch… See you soon!
Tigger

See photo of Hutch (Goldilocks) on my website:
www.dougcoxonline.com/mind-movies-photos

SCENE SIXTY-EIGHT

George

● ● ● ● ● ● ● ●

It was a wonderful invitation! A handful of radio and record executives were invited to the Hollywood Playboy Club, for a rather auspicious event. The Beatles were launching a new record label. You remember records... The large round disks of vinyl with a small hole in the middle. The gossip was, that one or more of the group would be in attendance. Naturally, I was in! During the cocktail reception, my friend and master promotion man, Don Grierson, gave me a wave and said to follow him. I did so and around the corner came face to face with George Harrison.

I have always been more interested in people than autographs, so after a warm and sincere handshake I asked, *"What is Apple Records all about and how may I contribute to its success?"*

It is amazing how an interest in others can spark a conversation and in this case a friendship. He explained that Apple Records was intended to become a birthing ground for new and promising artists. His eyes truly lit up when he began sharing with me, his passion for giving back and offering a chance to struggling artists.

Born in the same town as my dad, the youngest Beatle was an incredible composer and a gifted guitarist and vocalist. In our visits, following our first meeting, George Harrison proved to be as sweet and kind a man as his songs. *"My Sweet Lord…"*

Tigger

SCENE SIXTY-NINE

Moments

● ● ● ● ● ● ● ●

The last of the sliced and ziplocked turkey is placed upon my sandwich and the cranberry sauce is down to a few drops of luscious red juice on the crystal serving dish. For most of us, the holidays are a wonderful time of year. For some, time and circumstance create a bittersweet and melancholy sense.

I am often asked, *"How can I be cheerful in this contentious world?"* I learned, long, long ago, that I have no business attempting to enforce my happiness and sense of celebration on others but remember having been visited by life's greatest tragedies; I can only share my own journey into the light. Along with the divine guidance that moves ahead of me on the seas of life, I have chosen to be the master of my ship, the captain of my destiny and the navigator of my voyage!

To this end, I have inscribed on the first page of my charts, three principles that have given me the best opportunity to find joy in even the most severe of life's storms: First, I find the best that history has to offer, by *"Treasuring fond memories!"* It is my choice to focus my memory on the glories of my past. Next, I choose to *"Look with hope to the future!"* By believing in a positive view of what is yet to come, I sail a more enthusiastic course. And finally, I *"Believe in this Moment!"* because it is the only time in which I shall exist. I find that little slices of life are simply more manageable. I care about you and your times and my handful of *"Humbug"* friends and family, whom I adore! Happy, hopeful Holidays!

Tigger

SCENE SEVENTY

The Promise

● ● ● ● ● ● ● ●

A simple candy cane… A herders crook, a decoration for Christmas trees, a sweet treat for children of all ages. A symbol of the shepherd in all of us!

Many years ago, on the sage of a frozen, windswept, snowy plain, a shepherd huddled deep into his bedroll. Tired from a long day of caring for his flock, he was trying to keep from freezing to death. As the 50 degrees below zero wind howled across him, he thought, *"this is certainly a God forsaken place!"* As soon as the thought rolled across his mind, he knew better and changed his lament into a dream and a prayer. *"If I survive this night,"* he prayed, *"I will return here and build a refuge for other shepherds that may pass this cold and lonely place."*

Today one of the famous Little America Hotels sits on that sight. Food and warmth and comfort for a weary traveler.

Their motto: *"A promise kept, a dream fulfilled!"*

May we all become better shepherds of our families, friends and neighbors!

Meet me in Montana!
Tigger

SCENE SEVENTY-ONE

Anticipation

● ● ● ● ● ● ● ●

Daylight Savings, love it or hate it, here it is again! As my faithful readers are aware, each Easter, we gather family and friends from around our beloved America and head for Carmel-By-The-Sea, in California. I am cherishing every moment leading up to the arrival of each guest. What a wonderful celebration of our mental capacities, that we can love the adventure in advance, in the moment of its occurrence and then in the memories thereafter. As Carly Simon sings, *"Because these are the good old days!"*

Where are you heading in the days and weeks to come? Who will be there with open arms to greet you? How do you picture the place and the people and how vividly do you remember the sounds and smells of your past adventures. I love to live 100% of this marvelous life and to do so, I must wring every moment of joy out of not only, the when but the *before* and *after* of my events.

In my anticipation, I see you now. In joy I will greet you then and in wonder, I will treasure the moments and memories of our time together!

Tigger

SCENE SEVENTY-TWO

Bathed

• • • • • • • •

Above the beautiful little city of Saint George, in southern Utah, there is a trail that leads up to the top of a rugged escarpment. Along with my dear friend, Jason Horn, my kids and I have named this place, *"The End of the World."* From this precipice, you can look out to the south and west, over the Virgin River and out across the huge and barren badlands of Nevada. This is not a journey for the faint-of-heart.

To make the climb, you must rise up from the valley, into a series of deep ravines, filled with huge boulders and wonderful strange vegetation. Eventually the hike turns into a scramble and then a rock wall climb that leads out onto a very thin path, traversing the very face of the End of the World. At the top, we have experienced rain, lightning, thunder, wind storms and more than once, a snow squall has driven us into a natural cave, where we built a fire to shelter out the weather.

Through sunrises, sunsets and starlit nights, from our rugged vantage point, we have been bathed in the wonder of nature. It is a magic place, where I find inspiration for my books and presentations.

In nature lies the regeneration of the human mind, spirit and soul!

Tigger

SCENE SEVENTY-THREE

Brand

● ● ● ● ● ● ● ●

At the westernmost edge of the Las Vegas Valley sits the *"Sandstone"* ranch. The *"Sandstone,"* established in 1876, it is a rare treasure in a world of encroaching cement, glass and noise. Before becoming a working cattle ranch, it was a campsite for Indians, outlaws and mountain men. Today it is a State Park and during my recent visit, standing on the original ranch house porch, looking out on the red rock escarpment, the history and the stark beauty of this place reminds me of just how important a brand is.

Each of us belongs somewhere; a family, a church, a synagogue, a temple, a service organization or for those of us who are employed, a company. Once we put our gear down in the bunkhouse and accept our first meal in the cook shack, we have made a promise to "Ride for the Brand!" From that moment on, every word we speak, every step we take, everything we do, we are riding for the brand.

Wherever you *"belong"* right now, if you ever find yourself, for whatever reason, slacking off, thinking badly or speaking badly about your *"Brand,"* you need to saddle up and take a long ride out to the foothills, listen to the desert wind and think about where you are, how fortunate you are and if perhaps you might need to adjust your grip on the reins.

To a cowboy, the invitation to hang your hat with an outfit, is an honor, an opportunity and a commitment to loyalty. You can count on me…

We Ride Together!
Tigger

SCENE SEVENTY-FOUR

Nose-Knows-No's

● ● ● ● ● ● ● ●

Sequoia, Carquinas, Turnagain, Walden, Nepenthe, Yost Van Dyke and The Baths, Two Medicine, Ayala Cove, Yankee Point, The Weirs, Waimanalo, Bondi and the Firehole… These are names you may not know, places that you may have never been but they live inside my spirit sense. It was my great fortune to have visited all of these places and a thousand more. The fragrance and perfume of them is an olfactory imprint that can never be separated from my being.

Our deepest sense of memory is the gift of smell. You are a travel agent too! Take a moment now and still your busy mind and think back to the places you have been and the experiences you have shared and then remember the fragrance and the perfume of those times. Campfires, s'mores, fresh-cut lawns or a holiday kitchen, they all belong to you.

No, I can't go there today. No, I can't go there tomorrow. I may never get there again but I will always be able to visit there in my senses. Right now, in my precious memory, I think that I will climb up on the John Deere and finish plowing this field for Mr. Clifford. The coastal earth furrows, smell like heaven and the strawberries and artichokes will taste twice as sweet.

You coming…
Tigger

SCENE SEVENTY-FIVE

Offshore Breezes

● ● ● ● ● ● ● ●

His name was Hobie Alter. He was both a dreamer and a doer! His *"Dreamsheet"* was clear: *"I want to make a living without wearing hard sole shoes or working East of California's Pacific Coast Highway."* (PCH-101) When the afternoon offshore breezes on the California Coast, blew-out the waves for surfing, Hobie created new "toys" for us to play with, on both land and sea.

The *"Henry Ford"* of surfing leaves behind Surfboards that we could afford and easily carry to the beach, along with paddleboards, kayaks and catamarans that scream across the top of the water. He also left us a joy for living, that perhaps only surfers can understand.

Hobie Alter was a *"Waterman"* and that is a title that all of us who rode and still ride today, wish to earn in our lifetime.

May it be said of us, either east or west of PCH, that

we dream, imagine, engineer and create our hearts desire.

And for heaven's sake may we have fun doing what we choose to do with our lives. *(In loving memory of Hobie Alter 1933-2014)*

Aloha Hobie,
Tigger

SCENE SEVENTY-SIX

The Sixth Sense

● ● ● ● ● ● ● ●

Found: For a newborn, 60,000,000 mind circuits open immediately and reach out, trying to see, smell, taste, touch and hear everything around them... A *child's* sense of wonder is what drives little hands and miracle minds, to reach out into the world. The gift of exploration!

Lost: Sadly, for a whole generation of children, technology and media are slowly destroying that sense of wonder and the experience of childhood. Because violence, sexuality, abuse and excess are exposed in a steady, vivid stream, there is nothing left for a developing mind to wonder about. No image, once seen can ever be unseen... It can only be buried!

The joy of finding love and the breathless racing of young hearts, has been lost to the ages. We no longer hold hands, we clutch PDA's.

Encourage the sense of wonder. Be a guide and parent

now, while there is time. Do it well and you will be friends with your offspring forever.

Tigger

SCENE SEVENTY-SEVEN

Voices

● ● ● ● ● ● ●

Hope for our beloved snowbound friends… Although our calendar says *"midwinter,"* I hear on the Desert Wind, a faint, sweet and wonderful sound. Our quail are awakening from their slumber and beginning to coo to one another. *"Chiquita-Chiquita,"* they sing. Outside our front door, at 5 am, while the great horned owls are still calling to each other, there is a rustling in the sagebrush and I am greeted by a brand new *"herd"* of bunnies. Yes, that's right; a family of rabbits is called a herd. Our cottontails are small with puffy white tails and the first rays of morning sunlight, through their new little ears, shines pink. These creatures are a joy to both our ears and our eyes. Why don't we view human creatures with the same joy and anticipation? Maybe because it's election season.

I have both friends and colleagues that give me this same lift and exuberance every time I see them in the hall, at the airport or on the trail. I want to be that guy! The one you look forward to seeing. I'd like to be the dude who brings a little springtime into the room and on departure, the soul who leaves a smile behind. I know that this cheerful behavior drives some people crazy but that is part of the fun and inspiration for the effort. I'm going to practice.

Hang on… Springtime is coming,
Tigger

SCENE SEVENTY-EIGHT

Forest Flower

● ● ● ● ● ● ● ●

If there was ever a place that deserves a treasured spot in your heart, *"Little Mountain,"* is that place. Whether you were introduced to this magical location on the silver screen or more recently on the national news, this was, is and will forever be a bit of paradise. For many years, this was my home. The beautiful Spanish word Montecito, means Little Mountain. Just now it would be hard to convince the residents that the name fits. As the flash floods came rushing down the naked earth left behind by the monster Thomas fire, it was as if the gods had unleashed an apocalypse of boulders, trees and mud as high as the second story of these magnificent homes. Dwellings, memories and lives were swept away in a matter of moments; thank you for your prayers.

I have such wonderful friends who call Montecito and Santa Barbara home. Watching social media and awaiting news of their safety and well-being, is one of the hardest things I have ever done. Perhaps you know some of these residents by their fame and fortune. I want you to know them by the fact that their hearts are far larger than their bank accounts.

One day, in the very near future, up through the mud and destruction, new life will arise. One single forest flower will appear as the harbinger of the days to come. The beautiful saxophone spirit of Charles Lloyd will once again lead our hearts in the dance.

Tigger

SCENE SEVENTY-NINE

Script

● ● ● ● ● ● ● ●

Once, when I was in my late teens, an adult friend of my parents made an observation that changed my attitude, my direction and my life. Today I can't remember what I was bragging about but I know that I must have been boasting, because the memory, if not the content of that encounter, still makes me flush with embarrassment. This gentleman, whom I much admired, allowed me to finish my diatribe and then said calmly, *"Doug, if they were casting the lead in the story of your life, you wouldn't get the part."*

He caught me. I was trying to be a screenwriter, an actor and a director, all without the experience and wherewithal to fulfil any one of those roles. I have always been a good and faithful listener. I am also, it turns out, a good and thirsty student. In that moment, as the flush slowly drained from my face, I took a deep breath, swallowed my pride and asked, *"OK, how can I become a star in this movie of my life?"*

He removed the pipe from his teeth and spoke of observing, more than performing. He said that time and experience were the only acting coaches worth a nickel and that belief was the true power behind any great achievement. He finally made his point by letting me know that had he not believed in me, he would never have given a second thought to my outburst, nor would he have invested his time in formulating a response.

He placed his pipe back between his teeth and said, *"my boy, if you are going to be writing the story of your life, you damn sure better be holding the pen in your own hand!"* Obviously, I had a long way to go!

Still working on my script…
Tigger

SCENE EIGHTY

The Truth

● ● ● ● ● ● ● ●

Look to the skies! Have you seen the Cosmic Lantern? It seems that we earthlings have a tendency to look at the world through old glasses. We've been where we've been, we've seen what we've seen and we know what we know or more accurately, what we have been taught. *"That,"* we say, *"is that!"*

Einstein suggested, *"Imagination is more important than knowledge; for knowledge is limited, whereas imagination embraces the entire world, stimulating progress, giving birth to evolution."* Perhaps it is time for us to set for ourselves a New Year's *evolution.*

For many of us, as we age, our views and therefore our attitudes begin to change. At the moment, when our curiosity should be reaching its peak, it seems that many folks I meet, are beginning to converse in terms of dead ends, instead of open roads. Is there life other than our own in the vast universe? Yep. Are we visited from time to time by interstellar craft? Yep. Is there, at this moment, an asteroid lining up its orbit to cross our own? Yep. Is there, in fact, a Cosmic Lantern, is sending forth images that will help us understand the fate of the universe? Yep.

So many wonderful possibilities are here awaiting the capture of our imagination. The choice is ours: are we, at whatever age, awakening or nodding off? We must, in this wonderful time of opportunity, re-awaken our need for information education and adventure. It's out there…

Tigger

SCENE EIGHTY-ONE

T-i-double-G-er!

● ● ● ● ● ● ● ●

I loved my work with the Seminole Tribe of Florida! As we began to grow from three thousand to ten thousand Team Members throughout the huge state of Florida, the brass wanted to know how I would be able to fulfill my duties as Director of Team Member Communications, across all those miles. I had no intention of doing it on my own, was my answer. We created a group of ambassadors that would be my eyes, ears and voice on the six properties. These marvelous leaders, from a variety of departments, were bright, intuitive and absolutely committed to their assignment.

During one of our ambassador summits, which we rotated between the properties, the group observed me bouncing up to the head of the conference table and our Tampa Ambassador, Deanna, exclaimed *"Oh my, you are TIGGER!"* and the name stuck.

Many of these terrific liaison members still work with the Tribal Casinos and the Hard Rock properties. All of them, wherever they may be today, remain heroes, sheroes and friends across the country.

These wonderful people made me look very good, Tigger

SCENE EIGHTY-TWO

Fire

● ● ● ● ● ● ● ●

I was never a really good student. One day my college biology professor invited me into his lab after school. I was nervous. He brought me over to his demonstration table and proceeded to pour out, onto the desktop, the contents of three, what appeared to be, empty beakers. To my amazement the top of the desk burst into flames. *"Wow!"* I exclaimed, *"What was that?"* He replied, *"A question… I can't believe it!"* He was referring to the fact that I had spent most of the first semester in his class without ever asking a question. My grades showed it. I was getting a *"D"* and he pointed out to me that it was not because *"D"* was my first initial.

Have you ever looked at your performance in life or in business and thought to yourself, *"I can do better than this!"* Look at your place on the scoreboard. Are you proud of your ranking? Or are you honestly better than that? Perhaps the answer is just a question away. *"How can I do better, be better, perform better?"*

We are surrounded by some of the very best minds available; friends, family, coworkers and people that share your community. All you need to do, is put away your fear of hearing the answer and ask for help, ask for guidance and then act on what you hear…

I did that day and the answer to my second question changed the direction of my life for all time. *"How did you do that?"* I asked in reference to the pyrotechnics on the desk. My professor answered, *"It's called FLASHPOINT… and it happens whenever all of the elements come together. What once was invisible, bursts into flame."* *"In nature"* he went on, *"it is always by accident. In life it is always by design."*

Tigger

SCENE EIGHTY-THREE

Ghost Service

● ● ● ● ● ● ● ●

Not a misprint… Though one of my favorite subjects has always been *"Guest Service,"* I have often brought to light the fact that companies seem to hire the dead to wait on guests and customers… This is a true ghost story. I was flying out of the Las Vegas airport. It was a busy day with a terminal full of folks scurrying to get in and out of town. When I examined my boarding pass, I realized why security had taken so long this time. My TSA-Pre number was not on my document. *"Known fliers,"* as we are called, are given some special perks. Light jackets and shoes remain on and we are sent to a very short cue for screening. I spotted a Southwest agent and asked if he might assist me in putting my ID on my boarding pass. His response was immediate: a big smile, a friendly voice and a positive greeting. He stopped what he was doing and got to ticking away on the computer. *"Sorry, Mr. Cox"* he said, *"your number was not entered into your profile. But you're all set now! Anything else I can do?" "Just one thing,"* I replied, *"let me know how to tell your company about what a great job you are doing." "I'm Ronald," he replied. "Just tell them Ronald at McCarren. Everybody knows me."*

On my return flight I went right away to a gate agent and asked to see Ronald. The lady had worked there for 11 years but did not know a Ronald. I covered the whole C concourse, searching for someone that knew Ronald. No luck. Perhaps that is because his name was "Donald" and he was fantastic!

Thank you Donald and Southwest,
Tigger

SCENE EIGHTY-FOUR

The Sale

• • • • • • • •

In 1949, long before my readers were going to the theater or many even born, *"The Death of a Salesman,"* was written by Arthur Miller. The story won a Pulitzer Prize and the play garnered a Tony for the best play. Both well deserved!

All of my life I have been a salesman. From newspapers door to door, to gasoline from the pump, stocks and bonds out of my briefcase, clothing off the rack, records and music out of my heart and shampoo out of my soul, I have been a salesman and proud of it. In the last few days I have had the opportunity to re-connect with one of the best executives I have ever known. Over our first meal together in many years, we both spoke of our friendship and its resilience. Against the odds and the fates, we have never left the human connection behind.

Whenever we met, we were always competitors selling our ideas and our products, one against the other.

Over our recent first sip of wine, my faithful friend commented that as tough as things got and as much as we wanted the business at the moment, we never did or said anything, to get that business that might have torn our friendship apart.

Perhaps we and our leaders might well take a lesson from two long time pitchmen, in selling in and closing the greatest sale of all… A lasting friendship!

Tigger

SCENE EIGHTY-FIVE

Shhhhh

• • • • • • • •

We are on the set of a major film production. I can't tell you what it is, because then I would have to ask you to keep it a secret and you know how that ends up! In the audience of the huge casino ballroom, there are about 1500 people. Extras, the movie folks call us. We are moved around to suit the scene being filmed and then told to sit and wait. During the "sit and wait" period everything starts out quiet and still but then the volume of the 1500 restless voices begins to rise. The director, trying so hard to converse with his production team, finally grabs a microphone and whispers *"shhhh..."* To which everyone quiets down for a few moments. But then, the game starts all over and over, all day long.

I wanted to tell the director, that if he had just told the extras why he needed their cooperation, the silence would have lasted far longer. As Viktor Frankl, the great logo therapist and concentration camp survivor taught, when we have a *"why"* for which to live, we can bear almost any *"what or how…"*

It is in silence that we hear the true magic…

I'm listening,
Tigger

SCENE EIGHTY-SIX

Suite One

• • • • • • • •

In the late nineteen-sixties, my friend Steve Harris, from Electra Records, called me on a sunny, Southern California Friday afternoon. He told me that he was doing a favor for a friend and asked if I would be willing to help. This is one very good guy, so my answer was yes. I met him in a parking lot in Hollywood, jumped into his shiny, black, hot little *"record guy"* convertible and we took off for my unknown destination.

We soon left the main drag and with radio station KRLA blasting, we headed up one of the famous canyons in the Hollywood Hills. In short order we whipped into the driveway of a *huge* mansion. Steve informed me that we were going to bunk here for the night and then head out on our adventure in the morning. As we stepped through the palatial front door, I asked, *"Where are we? Whose place is this?"* He just replied, *"look through that door and you tell me..."* One glance through the door and I knew. An array of immaculate very high powered sports cars filled the huge garage but the Porsche nearest to me was a sure give-away. This was Steve McQueen's home.

It was huge, elegant and beautiful. Now, a *"Suite"* is a collection of musical performances, strung together to create a whole symphony. In this case it is a collection of stories, each requiring their own space for the telling… So stay tuned for next week's Desert Wind…

More to come…
Tigger

SCENE EIGHTY-SEVEN

Suite Two

• • • • • • •

Next morning, at sunrise, I took one last peek into that garage before we drove away. It was not a dream. It was still there, looking and smelling expensive and powerful! Back in the black sports car, the information on our secret mission was still coming forth, painfully, slowly. I was to get on a United flight from LAX to SAN (San Diego) and then await the arrival of the next flight from San Francisco. In those days we were allowed to meet the airplane on the tarmac. I was to wait at the bottom of the air-stairs and all would be revealed to me.

The 727 taxied over and as the stairs were rolled into place, I took my station, as assigned. At first the passengers exiting the aircraft were unfamiliar but then one that I recognized stepped out on to the boarding stairs. It was a pretty, young lady with huge, wild hair, blowing in the bay breeze. She looked around at the faces below and then headed down the stairs, directly toward me. *"Are you Doug Cox,"* she asked. *"Yes ma'am,"* I replied and she handed me a carryout cup, straw and all! *"I understand that you like these,"* she offered, smiling. I took a sip. She was right. It was a perfect, chocolate milk shake, delivered by non-other than Judy Collins, the famous songbird with the magnificent voice.

She had come to San Diego to promote her newest record and Steve knew that I would escort his artist to all of the radio and television stations, making her introductions. Oh yes… Judy's other name: Judy Blue Eyes, made famous in the Crosby, Stills, Nash and Young recording of "Suite: For Judy Blue Eyes…"

I never even noticed that I didn't meet Steve McQueen…

Tigger

SCENE EIGHTY-EIGHT

Down Under

● ● ● ● ● ● ● ●

My journey, from Monterey California to Sydney Australia, was a long one, twenty-one hours and two stops. My first seminar was to be held in Melbourne and so I raced through each airport to catch my flight.

Once in my hotel room, in Mel-Bun as it is pronounced, in *"Strine,"* (Australian) I could look across the beautiful downtown park. Through the trees, I caught a glimpse of what looked to be a Ferris wheel. You would never guess it but I love people and fun! Sounds like a carnival to me, so I hit the elevator, crossed the quiet street and headed out through the park. Although the park seemed empty, I heard the sounds of someone laughing in the branches above me. Strange, because it was Tuesday and the park was empty but the sounds persisted. There it was again! Some bloke was up there laughing! T'was no doubt that the sound was coming from the tree branches above me but who, where and how?

At last I noticed a strange bird perched about 15 feet above my head. I grabbed my camera and as I was snapping away, the critter began to call out and it was then that I realized who was laughing at this yank. It was a kookaburra Bird, a native of Australia and the joke was on me.

Google this wonderful bird and listen to its infectious laughter.

G'Day Mate,
Tigger

SCENE EIGHTY-NINE

Slack-Key

● ● ● ● ● ● ● ●

Tonight, between the beautiful sands of Waikiki beach and the "House without a key," on the patio of the world renowned Halekulani Hotel, there is music in the glorious island sunset. *"Sweet dreams Mapuana... Hawaii smiles on you..."* At one time, in the early 20th Century, Hawaiian music became very popular on the *"mainland,"* as the 48 states were called. Steel guitars blended with the beautiful voices of island people, to create a picture of paradise with swaying palm trees and graceful dancers, painting the lyrics with their hands and bodies. As it was, and will be again tonight, this is public-tourist music. It is sweet and wonderful in its style but in those days, in the homes and on the back porches of the islands, a very different, very personal type of music was being played. It was known as *"Slack-Key,"* and it was played unamplified with voice and songs in pure Hawaiian.

The term, Slack-Key, *(kī hō'alu)* refers to the open

tuning or *"slacking"* of two or more of the guitar strings, to produce a finger-picking style that was truly suited to the back-yard dancing and singing of families and friends. You may Google *"Kaliponi Slack Key"* by Keola and Kapono Beamer and you shall hear it.

Better still, bring your ukulele down to the beach and I will tell you the story of how the music found its way from Gabby Pahinui and the paniolos, out to the world.

"One kiss of sweet aloha, aloha I love you…"
Tigger

SCENE NINETY

Walkabout

● ● ● ● ● ● ● ●

As he stopped the car, my friend asked, *"Do you want a ride back to the hotel or would you like to spend the day here at the beach?"* My response was instantaneous. *"Leave me here. I'll find my way back to Sydney!"* It was my first tour of Australia, the land down under and I wanted to get my fill of this wonderful place and these terrific, colourful people. At the moment of my response, I had not considered the distance from Bondi Beach to the Menzies Hotel in downtown Sydney but I didn't care. This was my golden opportunity to walkabout the 5.6 miles back to my room! Six glorious hours…

From my wonderful time on the beach, to the whole of the journey, I can tell you now that I enjoyed every sunny mile. From bar-keepers to dry cleaners, from quickie marts, to service stations, the smile and the greeting were the same. *"Where do you hail from yank?"*

Beginning with a burger at The Stuffed Beaver and a fine cocktail at the Bucket list, to milk bars and servos, I walked into every place along the way, just to say howdy! The moment the storekeeper heard my greeting, they would raise a hand and say, *"Howdy Yank!"* I found an uncommon courtesy in every face and every word I encountered along my way.

Tigger says, why ride when you can walk... Or bounce!

SCENE NINETY-ONE

Mountain Light

● ● ● ● ● ● ● ●

To the west of our home, reaching up into the blue southwestern sky, there stands a rock escarpment. On winter afternoons, when the shortened day is over and the southern sun begins to set behind her rugged cliffs, there is a moment where a crack, between two huge boulders, allows that light to shine hazily through. I have often climbed to that spot, just below the rim, in the hopes of encountering the "thrush" that was instrumental in guiding Bilbo *Baggins and the dwarves in their quest to destroy "Smaug,"* the mighty dragon.

The moon writing on the map, directed: *"Stand by the grey stone when the thrush knocks."* This was a sign that the keyhole to the secret door was about to reveal itself. Once high summer returns, it is my intention to be present, in the moment foretold, to feel the bright ray of the blinding sun take me full in the face and illuminate for me, the doorway to even greater adventures.

Have you forsaken adventures? Have you cast aside your dusty old bound classics and given up your childlike sense of wonder? There is a great difference between childlike and childish. May you always keep the one and let go the other. Young in heart, mind and spirit… Forever!

Tigger of Middle Earth

SCENE NINETY-TWO

Allouette!

● ● ● ● ● ● ● ●

On the wall, above and behind my desk, there hangs a wonderful painting, by *John Ford Clymer.* The bold artwork reveals to us, a gathering of mountain men dancing around a campfire, at their winter rendezvous. The artwork is entitled; *"Allouette"* (Pronounced roughly, All-Wet) and these rugged men are obviously singing a French-Canadian folk song, to accompany their celebration at having survived another brutal season in the highest country of North America.

In my childhood home, singing at the dinner table was a nightly feature. Songs in languages, other than English, were a mainstay of our meals and also our introduction to a few words in the dialect of distant places. As kids will do, I misheard the lyric and for years sang, *"Allouetta, jaunty allouetta…"* I loved the term *jaunty* without knowing why, until I read the definition some years later; *"Having or expressing a lively, cheerful self-confident manner!"*

The creators of Bugs Bunny, Tom and Jerry and many more, obviously agree, as this song appears often in their fabulous cartoons and shows. In a world grown so contentious, I picture, as I climb my mountain, my brothers in arms singing along, in a language made common by our battles, as we march out to defend our mutual freedoms. *"Allouette, gentile Allouette, Allouette, je te plumerai!"* Now you sing it with me! I promise that someone in your family knows this song.

Jaunty seems to describe perfectly a certain Winnie-the-Pooh character. Now let's see… Who could it be?

SCENE NINETY-THREE

Remembered

● ● ● ● ● ● ● ●

In the afternoon light, the view across the valley seems to go on forever. I've got a lot of living to do but I know that life, like the day, does not go on forever. I know because I lost a friend recently and I remember vividly a conversation that we had about memories.

We had done so many things together, rode so many trails, and lived so many adventures, that we had pretty much emptied out our bucket list before his unexpected passing. Our conversation played a prominent role in the crafting of my book, *"SH-Boom."*

With no foreknowledge of his impending fate, he asked me how I wanted to be remembered. My answer was, "I really never thought about it!" He let on that he wished he had saved more to leave behind. Beyond that, he wanted to leave a legacy of his history, both accomplishments and failures.

He was going to start a journal to capture the story of a life… His! He finally admitted that he just didn't know where to begin. I wrote my book with my friend in mind. With every word and page, I was creating a guidebook for the preparation of a legacy, a history of the struggles and the glories of a lifetime.

There is more to your life than you would ever imagine. Begin your journal today.

Tigger

If, perhaps you wish some guidance on the adventure, go to www.dougcoxonline.com/sh-boom and we will make the journey together!

SCENE NINETY-FOUR

Mind Movies

● ● ● ● ● ● ● ●

"A fiery horse with the speed of light, a cloud of dust and a hearty Hi-Yo Silver, The Lone Ranger rides again!" Every Saturday afternoon of my childhood, he rode out of my radio and into the theater of my mind. With his faithful friend and companion Tonto, the Lone Ranger was my hero!

Is there a movie, television show, a piece of music or an individual, that has left a lasting impression on you? When you are called upon, in an emergency or during a family, community or national crisis, what words, what voices, what beliefs and memories flow through your spirit to reaffirm your power, strength and leadership?

The announcer always reminded us that, *"The daring and resourceful masked rider of the plains, led the fight for law and order in the early west!"* It was clear to me that I sure wanted to grow up daring and resourceful. In putting out a brushfire, rescuing a drowning boy scout or shepherding our family through an incredible tragedy, my collection of heroes, sheroes, both real and created have made a difference in my life. Their courage and wisdom have left me with a saddlebag full of thoughts to call upon, when the opportunity arises.

Today, as I travel the world, sharing the message of dreams, belief and hope with thousands of friends and audience members, I still ask myself: *am I truly committed and prepared to be daring and resourceful, in my ride across the plains of life?*

Let's Ride…
Tigger

SCENE NINETY-FIVE

Seiichi *Say-ee-chee* Part One

● ● ● ● ● ● ●

For those who have eyes, the world is full of adventure. Some years ago I received the gift of managing a radio station in San Francisco. During the first of each week I would provide leadership for our southern California station and then mid-week return to my post in the city by the bay.

On the evening of my first arrival for my duties in SFO, I stepped out of a taxi at what would become my bi-weekly home, The Miyako Hotel in Japan Town. The first face to greet me was that of the bellman; bright, cheerful and traditional Japanese. It was my honor to make the acquaintance of Sheiishi Tanaka.

My weekly visits to the beautifully decorated hotel, gave me the opportunity to get to know Tanaka-san and share with him my love for and curiosity about things tradionally Japanese. After three months, on one cold and rainy evening, I responded to a knock at my door, only to find my new friend standing in the doorway.

With a swift and courteous bow he simply said, *"Cox-san, tonight, you come, Buddhist church!"* With that simple command he turned and hurried away.

I could not have imagined the wonder that was about to unfold in my life.

In *part two,* come away with me to *"The dojo"* and my journey into the drums of Japan...

Tigger-san

SCENE NINETY-SIX

Seiichi Part Two

● ● ● ● ● ● ● ●

The church, on my arrival appeared dark and closed tight. With my collar turned up against the wind and rain, I moved to the side of the building and found a stone stairway leading down to a lower floor and a huge hand hewn doorway. Nothing could have prepared me for what I experienced when I pulled open the portal.

I was engulfed by the sound of drums of all shapes and sizes, and the color, energy and mastery of the drummers in motion. The sensei leading it all, no longer in his bellman's uniform, was my friend Seiichi-san, the *Grand Master of Kumidaiko,* or taiko drums.

Seiichi taught me, that in Japan, things are not rushed. They are allowed to grow, to develop and to take on the flavor of those committed to the experience. That is why he waited three months before inviting me to his Taiko Dojo and why he watched me carefully each week, for another three months before inviting me to join in.

This evening as I sat on the floor, legs crossed enchanted, the Master stood before me, drumsticks in hand and simply bowed slightly. It was an invitation that I treasured, as I do my friendship with the great Seiichi…

Domo Arigato, Sensei,
Tigger-san

SCENE NINETY-SEVEN

First

● ● ● ● ● ● ● ●

It is autumn… For many, this is a melancholy time, to look back and remember, often wistfully. Don't get me wrong, I love and treasure my memories. I'm just hooked on this moment and all the moments yet to come. Instead of *"lasts,"* I love to celebrate *"firsts."* I love the ballet of the first leaf to fall, in what will become a leaf-storm of beautiful color and magic. I anticipate the fragrance of the first pumpkin pie, fresh from the oven. I await the first family member to cross our threshold for a hug, a smile and a joyful homecoming. My heart is already packed for my first airport or train station greeting in your hometown.

All these things we have done before. All these moments are saved in the bank account of my soul. It is time now for us to remember forward and to draw out the interest on these magic firsts, before they become lasts!

Treasure fond memories, look with hope to the future

and believe in this moment, for it is the only thing that we possess…

Tigger

SCENE NINETY-EIGHT

Inheritance

● ● ● ● ● ● ● ●

How often I have said, *"I did this"* or *"I did that?"*
The truth is, I-we don't do anything truly on our
own. We stand on the shoulders of so many who came
before us whenever we think, act or speak.

My good manners spring from the example of my dad,
Charlie, *"please and thank you."* My desire to overcome
my shyness and share myself in public, has been inspired
by my mother and her father Reverend Charles. My wish
to speak well and eloquently, comes from listening
to my older brother at our family dinner table. My
younger sister Susan is a musicologist par excellence
and has taken me off the beaten path and exposed me
to some wild and wonderful musical adventures. How
do I begin to thank those who came before, for this
incredible inheritance?

In the Native American style of artwork, seen on
the cover of this book, one mountain range behind
the other seems to fade the more distant it becomes.

My great concern is that with time, I-we might well allow this priceless appreciation to fade. So let us say it now... *"To all of you, both older and younger, including my marvelous children, thank you for all that you have shared, taught and acted out on the stage of life before me, inspiring me to think, act and speak as I do..."*

Bless you,
Tigger

SCENE NINETY-NINE

December

• • • • • • • •

What age were you when you first remembered feeling that twinge of excitement that came as the days, the weeks, the months and eventually the year, turned into December? The cold wind that visits from the north seems to carry with it the first hints of a thousand and one special nights.

It's a time when the aroma of things prepared for supper, have begun to change. From cookouts on the grill with burgers, potato salad and ice cream sundaes, to soups and stews bubbling and squeaking in the crock pot. Things served individually during the warmer days, now just seem to fit together in a medley of family dining. The array of things on the menu are wonderful when they are combined and simmering altogether.

At this time of year, my heart often reawakens to a fresh wish to see humanity preparing our minds, hearts and souls for the Holy Days to come. America was once known as the melting pot of the world. In this twelfth month of the year we will be sharing our home with both friends and family. We look forward to visiting our neighbors, to break bread, raise our glasses and share a hug. Whatever the differences in our opinions and beliefs, may the beautiful colored lights that magically appear during this special month, illuminate the best in our nation and the glory of our human nature.

Tigger Claus

SCENE ONE–HUNDRED

Christmas Kept

• • • • • • • •

I stood at the top of the stairs, still cozy in red flannel pajamas, hair tousled and eyes bleary from my repose. This was the day; the morning, the moment I had waited for, so long. To a barely five-year-old lad, the wait had seemed intolerable. From the room at the bottom of the stairs, the firelight flickered and danced toward me, casting shadows of images most mysterious. The lights on our Douglas fir, standing guard near the bay window at the front of our home, twinkled out our greeting to neighbors and to the world. Mingled with the smell of the oak-wood fire, the fragrant boughs sent forth an aroma as sweet as any forest. It was a Christmas morning in the Cox home; Joy to the world!'

It's been ten decades since that morning and still I can recall the glory of it all. I realize now that the greatest part of the adventure was and always will be, the anticipation of the advent. Captured in pictures and books, sung in carol's and wrapped in beautiful paper, the gift was always the love and kindness shared by family, friends and strangers alike. Through all of the years of seminars that I have had the joy of presenting, my partners and I always wanted that day, that event, to be Christmas for our Guests.

In the background, served with eggnog and Karen Carpenter, there is always, in our lives, the words of Scrooge, *"It's not too late, I haven't missed it!"*

Merry Christmas Darling
Tigger

SCENE ONE–HUNDRED–ONE

Maria

● ● ● ● ● ● ● ●

The convention center was as noisy as only 10,000 hairdressers could be. Squeezed in between the pipe and drape of one little show room, we awaited the arrival of our brand new educator. Out from backstage he came. Sharp and handsome in a fine green gabardine suit. His tie was knotted perfectly and he was guiding a young lady before him. His model was blinded by her thick shampooed hair, combed to completely cover her eyes.

"Today," he shouted over the noise that surrounded us, *"I am going to cut the Maria. Do any of you know how to cut the Maria?"* he asked… No hands went up. He graciously placed his faceless model in his styling chair and then, in a gentle, powerful voice he repeated, *"Today I am going to cut the Maria"* and as his hands parted her long, wet hair to reveal her face, he concluded by saying, *"Because this is Maria!"*

To this day the hair on my arms stands up and the tears fill my eyes, as I recall that moment and my awakened understanding of how important we are as individuals. That great hairstylist, educator and friend, who shared his gift with so many of us was James Victor Junior. Jimmy left this world today and our loss is heaven's gain. I have no doubt that the angels will all look a bit more beautiful now!

Tigger

See photo of James Victor Jr., Doug Cox and Joel Gerson on my website:
www.dougcoxonline.com/mind-movies-photos

SCENE ONE-HUNDRED-TWO

Wild

● ● ● ● ● ● ● ●

As our southwestern winter turns slowly into spring, the creatures of the wild begin to find their voices. Just before dawn the great horned owls, who live just beyond our vision in the rocky cliffs, sing a song about rabbit stew to each other. The poorwills, or night jars as they are properly named, have just begun to call to one another in the darkness. First one voice and then another. In a week, the hills will echo with the chorus of their communication.

As the sun peeks over Doug's Mountain, from the top of our roof, our mockingbird begins calling hopefully, for a mate. We hope for his success because he will sing his lovesick song over and over until he finds her.

At one time there was a plan to build homes on the hills surrounding us. Had that happened, these wondrous voices would have fallen silent. We must find a balance between the needs (or desires) of man and the mysterious, primitive wild from which we have come. It is from this wildness that we draw our solace and maintain our sanity in a world trying so hard to go mad.

Come away with me…
Tigger

SCENE ONE–HUNDRED–THREE

California Dreaming

● ● ● ● ● ● ● ●

Aloha Friends and Colleagues:

My grandson's wedding was beautiful, and he and his bride were radiant…To attend the wedding, I flew from *"Desert Wind"* Country, to Sacramento California, at dawn, on a nearly empty 737. Once the aircraft was abeam the Sierras, I could look out my port window and down upon Sequoia/Kings Canyon National Park. The trees below me are the oldest living things on earth and they are so intelligent that they create their own unique fragrance and environment.

Next up, or *down* below me, is Yosemite Valley. A glacially carved, waterfall graced, canyon, that is so beautiful and majestic that it completely captivated both John Muir and Ansell Adams. Completing the trifecta, the aircraft banks left to begin its dissent into the San Joaquin Valley. I move to the right forward window seat and gaze down upon one of the most magical sights in the world, Lake Tahoe. It is a rich blue wonder of crystal clear snow melt. It shimmers like a turquoise stone, set in a ring of high sierra mountains.

Three words: Wild, pristine and magnificent! I have visited, backpacked, horse-packed and camped in and around all three of these wonders and I am still spellbound.

If you have not had the opportunity to experience these places, you must add them to your bucket list. Three more words… Plan, visit, stay!

See you on top of Half Dome.
Tigger

SCENE ONE–HUNDRED–FOUR

Cops

● ● ● ● ● ● ● ●

The first time I shook hands with Mark, we were watching the world champion Denver Broncos play a fine game of football. We cheered until we were hoarse. The next time we connected, he was standing behind the bar in a classy restaurant, mixing superior cocktails for the fine neighbors of Castle Rock, Colorado.

The third time we met, he took me outside to show off his new ride… Big bucks, big horsepower and classy, from bumper to bumper. Imagine my surprise, when during what seemed like a charmed life, he announced a major shift in his direction. *"Doug,"* he said, *"I'm going to apply for a job in law enforcement."* You know me. I believe a man can do anything with his life that he decides to! Thumbs up…

Next trip to the Rockies Mark was in the academy and too busy to get together, so imagine my enthusiasm when *this time*, a year later, I got to share a fine lunch with both my son Chris and Mark, a full-blown

Denver Sheriff's Officer.

Those of you who know me are aware of my deep respect for law enforcement and the men and women who serve so bravely behind the badge. Just double my pride for this young man who is on his way to a great new career protecting and serving. With officers like Mark on our side, we are a better place and a better nation.

Congratulations Officer Losciale!
Tigger

SCENE ONE–HUNDRED–FIVE

Elvis

• • • • • • • •

Martoni's restaurant in Hollywood was very dark. The stars like it that way, so coming in out of the afternoon sunlight, made it tough to make out faces. As I took my seat at the bar, I heard the voice: *"How's it goin'?"* he asked. Though I could not see, I could hear well enough and the voice was unmistakable… It was *The King! "Going good,"* I replied. I have had the gift of meeting many interesting people in my life and so I am never awe struck in those situations but I do want to make something out of those moments. So, rather than going for an autograph, I asked, *"What does someone like you think about most of the time?"* His response was immediate, gentle and complete… "I think about a lotta things," he began, *"I think about bringing some happiness to others and I want somehow to make the world a better place. I think mostly about bein' a good enough man one day to be a daddy."* Before I could gather my thoughts on how simple and profound his answer was, he turned right into my face and asked, *"What do you think about?"*

I was stunned! The only thing I could do was stammer out a repeat of what he had already said so clearly. My final comment was, *"I guessed that I would like to make the world a better place, but I could never do it the way that he could..."* He looked into my eyes and as he turned back to his drink he said, *"Not sitt'n in here you can't!"*

Those of you who know me well, are aware that I don't go into bars very often…Now you know why?

The next time I saw Elvis, he was coming down the trail toward me. He is a sweet, beautiful and well trained silver poodle. We always stop to visit and he reminds me of an afternoon many years ago in Hollywood, California when I met a singer with the same name.

I love Critters…
Tigger

See photo of Elvis on my website:
www.dougcoxonline.com/mind-movies-photos

SCENE ONE-HUNDRED-SIX

Patience

● ● ● ● ● ● ● ●

Since the moment a certain one of my photos was published, I have had so many great responses… Thank you for your questions. *"Where did you find this incredible whatever it is?" "How did you get so close to this magnificent dragonfly?" "How long did it take you to capture this magic photo?"* Following is the story of this wonderful piece of art.

I know that our friends, Tom and Donna, would never refer to their home as an estate, but that is exactly what it is. It is two stories of history and wonder and a yard that fills a whole California hillside. To capture my photographs, I use a technique which I refer to as, *"Hunting!"* I was out at dawn walking the property, when a flash of blue caught my eye. It was 6am and this *"Snake-Doctor,"* as they call them in the south, flew past me at light speed. I tried to follow him but to no avail. So I did what I often do and that is to sit down, start sending out vibes to my prey and then just wait. And wait. And wait.

Finally, dancing in on an afternoon shaft of sunlight, I was rewarded for my patience. It was 3pm, when down the long driveway he came, darting in-and-out of the bushes that line the entry. I waited for another hour while he finally found a resting place in the Oleanders and at last I moved in silently and went to work. From that moment until darkness closed in on this magic adventure, I did the easiest part of photography… From 6 inches away, I snapped the shutter… over 100 times. I must say that I loved the experience as much as I love the resulting photo!

Tigger

See photo of this dragonfly on my website:
www.dougcoxonline.com/mind-movies-photos

SCENE ONE–HUNDRED–SEVEN

Photos and Folks

● ● ● ● ● ● ● ●

My recent Facebook post of a photo with George Harrison got a lot of buzz. One of my friends wrote to say she loved the photo. I replied that a photo is just a photo but friends like her are a living treasure. She took me to task for my comment.

Cheryl explained that photos are so important, because they are a record of our history. They are the visual memories of our lives. As a photographer, I knew that she was absolutely right. My point was, that all too often, we wait until the passing of a friend or loved one, before we tell them how we feel. Gordon Lightfoot, who is very much alive, is a great example. I've been fortunate enough to tell him, personally, that I thought he was one of the greatest composer/ poets of our time.

When Gordon leaves this earthly plane, there will be a great outpouring about his passing and his powerful effect on music and word-painting. I wanted him to know it in his living years.

If you love a friend or a family member, teacher, coach or artist who has touched upon your life, tell them thanks today! Now I'm going to put on my headset and listen to *"Beautiful"* by Gordon Lightfoot…

Love you, Tigger

See photos of George Harrison and Gordon Lightfoot on my website:
www.dougcoxonline.com/mind-movies-photos

SCENE ONE-HUNDRED-EIGHT

Wings Two

● ● ● ● ● ● ● ●

There is nothing more inspiring than to look up in the cold grey winter sky and see a flock of wild geese passing over. Here, in the west, weather wise, our seasons don't always conform to what the rest of the nation is doing and so, for the last few weeks there have been long strands of wild-wings in the skies over head. The flight of waterfowl always indicates to me, either the end or the beginning, of a primal journey. They are either going to or returning from places familiar, over routes that require no compass or satellite guidance. Perhaps you live in an area where you have seen the long "V" formations overhead during migration.

As my Tribal friends have taught me, in life, as in business, understanding why things happen in nature can serve as a beneficial guide to harmony and increasing success. There are two main reasons that geese fly in formation. The first is the conservation of energy. Imagine flying a thousand miles or more each year. Each bird flying slightly above the one in front, decreases the wind resistance and allows for long periods of flight, without the need to stop and rest.

Geese, flying alone, have an increase in heart rate that requires more frequent stops to rest and a greater strain on their heart and health. The second reason for flying in formation is to keep track of every bird in the group. Communication and coordination are improved in this way.

Don't spend time worrying about your place in the formation...You too will be called upon to lead one day. Fly strong and true!

Tigger

SCENE ONE–HUNDRED–NINE

Bloodlines

● ● ● ● ● ● ●

In my office, at KRLA radio in Pasadena, California, the promotion man from Capital Records handed me an LP and said, *"you are probably the only radio man in America that will understand this."* I had always trusted Don Grierson, after all, he was the one who introduced me to George Harrison and so, without even looking at the cover of the recording, I slapped it on the turntable and dropped the needle right in the middle. *"I can't hold it on the road when you're sitting right beside me and I'm drunk out of my mind, merely from the fact that you are here…"* I was once again a teenager out on highway 99 in the San Juaquin Valley. John's was a rich, compelling voice and he sang as if perhaps he felt we were running out of time.

"Signals Through the Glass," was the album and John Stewart, late of the Kingston Trio, was the artist. On the cover, John quoted John Updike, *"We are all so curiously alone but it's important to keep making*

signals through the glass!" This was the beginning of a wonderful friendship. To have John and his beautiful, talented wife Buffy come for dinner, sit out by the pool and sing, *"The Pirates of Stone County Road,"* was a moment that I will treasure forever.

I was born in California and my bloodlines there run deep. Since I left radio, many years ago, I have been traveling throughout the world, sending signals through the glass.

Tigger

You can Google the song, "July You're a Woman" from the Phoenix Live LP and listen to it online.

SCENE ONE–HUNDRED–TEN

Beginnings

● ● ● ● ● ● ● ●

As this will become the final chapter (or scene) in my new book, it has great significance in the story. Although I have lived through many endings in my life, it is the birth, or re-birth of the *new*, that lights the fuse for my fireworks.

This last week we returned to the Spring Mountain Ranch Outdoor Theater, to enjoy another production. Turns out, it was something that proceeded the performance, that set my mind and spirit on a new and hopeful path.

With the hot early evening sun on our backs, the young military recruits presented our nation's colors to the sold-out audience. As the strains of our national anthem sprang forth from the heart and soul of the young female vocalist, the folks standing around me started to sing. It came slowly at first, as if no one was exactly sure what to do, what was right, what was politically correct. Well damned if the whole audience didn't eventually join in, creating a *"joyful noise"* that filled the air and echoed back from the mighty sunset-backlit mountains. I wonder what the animals and birds thought of this outpouring of spirit for our tattered nation.

And this, the final scene in my latest book, is not the end but simply the overture of an even more wonderful future story. With our faces turned to the warm *"Desert Wind,"* I realize that with all our many differences, we are fortunate Americans, one and all… I hope that you have enjoyed this book: *"Mind Movies!"*

We Ride Together,
Tigger

To my Readers

One cannot give a talk, compose a song or write a book like this without so many wonderful others. This is a tribute to two of my four legged friends, one living, one passed, who have shared the trail with me.

We have weathered some losses while writing this book
Both human and K-9 and feline just look
A tribute to two of my four legged friends
Who will walk by my side so the trail never ends

Let's start with Cabo who's nearly a horse
All he needs is a saddle and rider of course
When I call from my mountain a mile up above
Cabo comes running to share all his love

Now Cricket was truly the mayor of our trail
She wags her big heart now instead of her tail
Today at the top I look up from the ridge
And smile at my friend on the rainbow bridge
For my readers and fellow climbers, thank you!

I love you dearly,
Tigger

See photo of Cabo on my website:
www.dougcoxonline.com/mind-movies-photos

Made in the USA
Columbia, SC
20 November 2018